T5-AGN-883

A narrative of homosexual family values. The author, a gay male psychologist, passes the real-life test of finding a birthmother who would have the baby with whom he and his life partner, a gay male physician, would become permanently bonded in parenthood. An engrossing personal odyssey.

John Money, Ph.D.
Professor Emeritus of Medical Psychology and of Pediatrics
The Johns Hopkins University and Hospital

Enlightening and moving! *Getting Simon*, redefines "family values" in a way that will surprise and uplift the reader. If only all parents wanted their children as much as the author does.

Joshua Brand
Creator/Producer of Television's *Northern Exposure*,
St. Elsewhere, and *A Year in the Life*

A vivid and compelling account of one very personal journey to fatherhood, *Getting Simon* will prove to be an invaluable resource for the thousands of gay men who increasingly see fatherhood as an option in their lives.

And to those who say that homosexuals are causing the destruction of Family in America, I say, "read *Getting Simon.*" Every page demonstrates the care, planning, consideration, desire and unbounded love these men put into creating a family. Simon is a very lucky little boy—more children should be so blessed.

Tim Fisher,
Executive Director, Gay and Lesbian Parents
Coalition International

Getting Simon is a tale of cultural resistance—to prejudice, to sexism, to the presumed limits of (gay) male experience. It will become a critical document for future generations of men who not only have the courage to love other men, but who also wish to have children of their own.

Tony D'Augelli, Ph.D.
Professor of Human Development, Penn State University

Must reading for all, especially for those who appreciate strong family values. The concept of FAMILY transcends sexual orientation. This book is compelling evidence that wonderful parenting comes from *human* passion, be it gay or straight.

Noemi E. Masliah, Esq.
Co-Chair, Board of Directors
Lambda Legal Defense and Education Fund, Inc.

Until recently, the longings of openly gay men for fatherhood had to remain whispers in their souls. Kenneth Morgen has given us the moving story of his determination to fulfill his humanity. It offers inspiration and affirmation that love and dedication are the vital ingredients which define a family."

April Martin, Ph.D.
Psychologist and Author, *The Lesbian and Gay Parenting Handbook*

Getting Simon

Two Gay Doctors'
Journey To Fatherhood

Kenneth B. Morgen

BRAMBLE ❖ BOOKS
New York

For information write to:
Bramble Books, 8 Route 212, Bearsville, NY 12409

Library of Congress Cataloging-in-Publication Data

Morgen, Kenneth B.
    Getting Simon : two gay doctors' journey to fatherhood /
Kenneth B. Morgen.
        p.   cm.
    ISBN 1-883647-04-5
    1. Morgen, Kenneth B.—Family. 2. Westrick, Sam—Family.
3. Gay fathers—United States. 4. Gay parents—United States. 5.
Adoptive parents—United States. 6. Adoption—United States. I.
Title.
HQ76.13.M67 1995
306.874'2—dc20   95-13177
                                            CIP

Photo credit front and back cover: Michael Barge

First Printing 1995
1 3 5 7 9 10 8 6 4 2

Printed in the United States of America

The paper used in this publication meets the minimum requirements
of American National Standard for Information Sciences—Permanence of Paper
for Printed Library Materials, ANSI Z39.48-1984.

Dear Birthmother,
Thank you for making
my life complete.

Acknowledgments

This book is drawn wholly from my personal journal, which I kept during the years my life partner and I were trying to create a family. All of the characters and vignettes are true to life although most names, including our son's, and other identifying information have been changed to protect people's privacy.

For this gay man, the journey to parenthood was not as easy as planting a seed and watching it grow. During this journey, I encountered many detours. Usually they were dead ends, leaving me feeling frustrated and ever-increasingly in despair of succeeding. But along the way, lifting my spirits and my hope, were kind, helpful individuals who, like spectators at a marathon, cheered me through the roughest spots and encouraged me to persevere until my partner and I met our goal. These were people who believed that happy, healthy families come in a variety of configurations and who believed in Sam and me. It was their words of encouragement and advice that empowered me to sustain my search, and I would like to thank them now. Marla Hollandsworth, Ellen Callegary, Shelly Fingerhood, Linda Meade, Greg and Gail Alter, Lance and Lynda Luria, Maureen Kenny, Barbara Holtan, Fay Guss, Eugene Back, Claire Westrick, John Westrick, Dave Imre, Tom Crusse, April

Martin, the obstetrical nursing staff of Franklin Square Hospital who were so wonderful with two scared doctors, Clyde Tolley, who, through his organization, FACE (Families Adopting Children Everywhere), taught me Adoption 101, and the members of the Association of Single Adoptive Parents, who were so supportive of us at a time we needed encouragement most. Particularly, my respect and appreciation to Sally Arteseros, my editor, who brought order and rhythm to my private thoughts and feelings, Larry Bramble, my publisher, who believed that this story needed to be told and Lucille Guss, Lissie Waller and Donna Fox, who so generously gave of their time and literary skill in completing the final editing. And to the love of my life forever, Sam Westrick, without whom none of this would have been possible.

Ken Morgen
Hunt Valley
March, 1995

Chapter One

Dear Simon,

I write this to you with tears in my eyes. I love you so much and you're not even here yet. We've never met each other. I know you are out there and you're mine and you know I'm yours. Keep your faith; we'll find each other.

Love, Dad

Our desire to have a child started to become an obsession after a painful experience with a young woman (I'll call her Amy), who had wanted Sam and me to adopt the baby she was expecting. Sam was expressionless when he handed me the letter when I came home from work that evening. The envelope was enticing: "CONFIDENTIAL," it read. "TO BE OPENED BY DR. WESTRICK ONLY!" The words were in large block letters, commanding my attention. I opened the letter with trepidation. Even though Sam had briefed me on what to expect, my breathing was shallow and I was shaking inside. The handwriting was a neat, if immature script:

Dear Dr. Samuel J. Westrick,

Enclosed is a copy of my medical records from Community Hospital for June 10. I am well aware of the fact that you may not want to become involved with me again—but I wanted to write to you and ask if you are still considering adopting a baby. I am looking for good parents. I know I ran from you last time I was pregnant. I was scared. I lost the baby. This time I am still scared, but things are much better than before. 1) I have a therapist I've been seeing for a half year now and 2) the father of the fetus I am carrying is being supportive of my decision of an adoption.

I need to give up my job because it entails picking up heavy equipment and other things which could cause a miscarriage. So, I am going to need help with living expenses such as shelter, food, clothing, and medical and legal expenses.

I will understand if you don't want to become involved with me again. But I thought I'd ask you because you appeared very mature and like you would make an excellent parent. I don't have a phone—but the father of the fetus is Stuart Schwein. I don't want to call you because I am afraid to but I'll have Stuart call you on Monday June 25. Maybe you can talk. I'll have him call you at about 10:00 a.m. Thanks,

Amy Q.

Attached was a copy of the hospital emergency room progress note dated ten days earlier and the lab test showing that the serum pregnancy test on that day was positive. The words "Pregnancy" and "POS" on that note were circled, as if to prove that she really was pregnant. The doctor's chart note showed that she was approximately sixteen weeks along. He also noted a history of hospitalization for mental illness and a seizure disorder. The patient was discharged from the emergency room and encouraged her to start prenatal care as soon as possible and to keep in close contact with her therapist.

As I read the letter, I become heady with excitement and fear. We knew this woman. I first met Amy three years before. Her reappearance in our lives after all this time filled me with apprehension. My gut feeling was to throw the letter away and to urge Sam not to talk to her boyfriend. But Sam and I wanted a baby; how could we ignore any candidate? How many women had called or written offering us their babies? How many times would this happen again? At that moment, I felt this was our only chance to create a family for ourselves.

After our first meeting with Amy three years ago, we consulted an attorney and learned how independent adoption worked in our state. We asked Amy to fill out forms detailing her extensive medical and psychiatric history. She never completed them. We investigated her family of origin in an effort to determine her stability, but they stonewalled us. Despite our concerns about her integrity we came to realize that we, too, were desperate—desperate to have a baby.

I thought back to the first time I had met Amy. She had been a patient in the clinic where Sam worked as a medical resident. She had remembered him for his kindness. She had called him out of the blue, years after first meeting him, to say she was carrying twins. Did he know any gay couples who were interested in adopting? She was looking for a gay home because she was a lesbian. If she couldn't raise the babies, she would want a couple like herself to do so. We had always wanted children but never seemed ready until Amy called. We were so blinded by our desire, it did not even seem unusual that this self-professed lesbian was pregnant. We thought of this as a once-in-a-lifetime opportunity and that we'd better grab it before it passed us by.

We had several conversations with Amy during those early weeks of her pregnancy. Each one brought us a little bit closer to her and made the possibility of a successful adoption seem a little more promising. We were beginning to trust her. Then, one day, around the beginning of her second trimester, I called Amy. Instead of her voice or her answering machine, a recording told me that her telephone had been disconnected. There was no forwarding number. We wrote letters, but the mail was returned unopened, stamped: "Addressee moved. No forwarding address." Even her mother didn't know where we could find her. I was distraught. I felt as if our only chance at parenthood was lost forever.

For weeks after she disappeared, I mourned those twins, obsessed about where they were, where Amy was, and if we would ever hear from her again. I wondered if she had had second thoughts about giving her twins to two gay men, whatever their credentials. Unknown to us, this disappointment would be just the first in a four year string of heartbreaks along our journey to parenthood.

Here, today, turning over this letter to Dr. Westrick in my hands; reading the guilt and fear in the lines; considering the request for financial assistance; and noticing the conspicuous absence of any form of apology for abandoning us during the previous pregnancy, I wanted to throw the letter in the trash. I was angry and happy simultaneously. Was this a second chance at parenthood or an invitation to another disappointment?

We weighed the risks and benefits of getting involved with Amy again. Sam, patient and even-tempered as always, said he would talk to Amy's friend when he called. After much discussion, we decided that we would agree to adopt her baby, but that we would not get involved with Amy again until the month before she was due.

Amy's friend Stuart called the next Monday morning as expected. Sam told him that we would adopt their baby, that Amy should get good prenatal care at the family practice clinic where she was a patient and that she should call us one month prior to the birth so that we could make the necessary legal arrangements. He told Stuart that, given our experience with Amy three years earlier, we would neither give them money nor otherwise become involved in their lives until then. It was a relief to have decided not to become involved with them, although I knew that in the months to follow I would worry about how the pregnancy was going; where and with whom Amy was living; whether or not she was getting adequate prenatal care; whether or not she would change her mind about the adoption; and if she was healthy and safe.

Dubious of Amy following through, we managed to concentrate on our day-to-day lives. I was busy not only with my psychology practice but also with a political campaign supporting the passage of a local civil rights bill which included protection for gay and lesbian people, a half-time job for which I was the point man. My additional work on a community AIDS advisory board made distracting myself from thoughts of Amy and the baby fairly easy. Similarly, Sam was occupied with his medical practice, largely devoted to caring for people with HIV disease. Sometimes, privately, I wondered how we would be able to manage having a child with all of these demands competing for our time and energy.

By December, Amy was eight months pregnant. We expected to hear from her any day. By our calculations, the baby was due mid-January. I wanted to call, but we had no number. The first week in January passed with no word. I figured she had changed her mind and that we should give up hope. We assumed that if we didn't hear from her by the next week, we would abandon our hope.

On January fourteenth, seven months after she had mailed us her letter, Amy called Sam at his office. She told him she was due to deliver in three days! Did we still want her baby? Sam called me immediately. As he told me about their conversation, I observed that the good news was contaminated. Amy was now living in a motel and facing eviction for non-payment of rent. The baby's father was in jail. Amy was broke. As Sam spoke, I could feel myself getting sucked into her nightmare. We were about to learn the hard way that these were the riskiest circumstances under which to attempt a private adoption. Yet how could we turn down any chance, however slight?

After hanging up with Sam, I called our lawyer. She cautioned me about all the "red flags" she saw in this situation. It didn't take a rocket scientist to figure out that this would be an extremely high risk adoption. To say the least, she was unenthusiastic about advising us to go forward with it. Should we follow our hearts or our heads? We were paying dearly for her advice. What should we do?

Before we went to sleep that night, Sam and I decided to take our chances. I called Amy in the morning and gave her the names of the two lawyers given us by our attorney. Amy should choose one. We had our lawyer call the hospital to advise them of the adoption. Our lawyer warned us not to give her any money. All we could pay for were medical and legal expenses. The thrill of this impending birth was overwhelming. Throughout the day, between phone calls to the attorney, Amy, and Sam and seeing my patients,

I had a feeling of unreality. Could it really be true that we would be parents in less than five days? Where would the baby sleep? What would he wear? We didn't even have names picked out.

On the second evening after Amy's call, we met Amy at her motel. It was close to our home. Hauntingly reminiscent of our meeting almost four years earlier at her dark, depressing apartment, it was a dingy, soulless, sparsely furnished suite. The only sign of personal property was Amy's open suitcase on the floor. Clothes were scattered about, as if the room had been ransacked.

Amy was dressed in a stained sweatshirt and stretch jeans. Her long brown hair was oily and unkempt. Her round face was pale and her eyes darted frequently to the floor. She had trouble making eye contact. She sat on the edge of an old wing chair as we perched on the 50's style sofa; she didn't appear able to get comfortable in any position. It was thrilling to contemplate that the baby inside her might become ours.

In the two hours we spent together, she told us unflinchingly that throughout the term of her pregnancy, she had planned on our adopting this baby. She had been providing a safe haven for the baby - "your baby," she said. She shared that she had feared during the pregnancy that we would not be there for her as we said we would. "I know I'm irresponsible and can't take care of a baby...this is your baby inside me and you're going to get him soon," she whispered. Amy told us that she didn't want any contact with it or us after it was born; that she trusted us and knew that we would give it a good life. She let us know how hard it had been for her to resist the urge to call us. She could not explain why she did not call in December as she had agreed. When we left her room at eleven, we were elated yet uneasy, wondering if Amy was telling the truth and wanting more than anything to believe her.

The next day, Wednesday, Sam and I went to the library for books on parenting and and naming babies and to a store to shop for a layette. I had to laugh when I realized that even though I had a doctoral degree, I never knew what that word meant until now. We hadn't a clue as to what to name this child and were hoping that we could agree on at least one of each gender. Amy kept her appointment with one of the attorneys we referred her to, but she refused to sign release forms to release medical and psychological information. Another red flag hoisted. She said she wanted to tell her therapist about her decision first. Why would she say she wanted to go through with an adoption and then not cooperate with her lawyer?

At eight-thirty p.m. Amy called, sounding nervous. "I think I'm going into labor. Can you take me to the hospital?" I felt like every actor portraying an expectant father whose wife says, "Honey, I think it's time." I threw on my jacket and pushed Sam into the car. It took five minutes to get to the motel. She was waiting by the door with her suitcase, a huddled shadow in the night, clad only in jeans and that same sweat jacket too small to close around her swollen belly. I silently gave her credit for looking more calm than I did. On the way to the hospital, I called her attorney on my car phone, anxious about our reception at the hospital. There was no answer at her office. Frustrated, I mused lawyers didn't have to be on call like doctors. We had no idea whether the hospital had been alerted to receive two gay men escorting a woman about to have their baby, even if one of us was on the medical staff. Would we be able to witness the birth in the delivery room? Would the nurse place the baby on Amy's stomach after birth or take it to the nursery where we could hold it? Would we be able to feed and bathe the baby? Would Amy get the private room we planned so she wouldn't encounter another postpartum mother? We didn't want our birthmother having to watch another new mother cuddling her newborn and reminding Amy of her loss. Would these questions be answered in time?

It took half an hour to drive Amy to the labor and delivery area. Sam knew this hospital well. He gave it three years of his life as a family practice resident. As we accompanied her to the examining room, it became apparent that no one knew of her plan to give the baby up for adoption. This frightened me. The nurses were protective of Amy but allowed us to stay only because that was what she wanted. After Amy was hooked up to the uterine contraction and fetal heart rate monitors, we met her doctor, a third year obstetrics resident we later learned was a PLU ("People Like Us"—gay). Conspiratorially, she expressed happiness that Amy was going to give the baby up for adoption to us. I felt better knowing there was someone at the hospital who was sympathetic with our concerns—

and a lesbian. After waiting an hour, we were told that Amy was not in labor. We were instructed to go home and come back for antepartum testing the next day.

Before we went to sleep that night, the telephone rang. It was Amy. She said she was lonely and wanted reassurance that we would be there for her until the birth. However, her hidden agenda became obvious when she asked, "Can Stu call you collect from jail?" Not ten minutes later, the phone rang again. It was Stuart. He wanted to tell us that he supported Amy's decision about the adoption and would sign whatever papers we needed in order to for us to adopt their baby. Then, he asked, "Do you have three thousand dollars to post bond?"

Sam explained gently but firmly that we would accept and raise their baby. "The law prohibits adoptive parents from paying birth parents any money for other than legal and medical expenses," he said formally. "We can't give you any money." Stuart accepted that politely.

The next day Sam went to work as usual while I left at six a.m. to get Amy to the hospital for her antepartum testing. I learned antepartum was Latin for "before birth." At the hospital, Amy asked me to stay with her throughout the process, something I was grateful to do. Among other things, Amy had a sonogram. I stayed in the room with her for this procedure and was amazed at the complete little form on the television screen. I couldn't tell if it was a boy or a girl, but I was awestruck at the technology that allowed me to see my child before it was born. I was reminded of the final scenes of "2001: A Space Odyssey." This image on the screen was that of a fully formed human baby, curled up in an embryonic ball, floating peacefully in a warm, wet home, breathing fluid, unaware of the chaos going on outside. Soon, this little miracle would breathe air and I would be holding him in my arms. I ached so badly for this baby that I cried as I watched the screen. Amy clumsily tried to comfort me. The irony of the momentary reversal of our roles did not escape me.

From the sonographer we went to the uterine contraction and fetal heart rate monitors. That was when I had my first encounter with the hospital social worker. Ms. Bitt was a prim woman whose hair was short but soft-looking, belying the coldness with which she treated me. Ms. Bitt made no attempt to hide her shock at Amy's disclosure that she was going to give the baby up for adoption. I was dismayed that Amy's lawyer had not gotten through to the social worker yet. Practically none of the ground-laying which our lawyer said was so essential to a smooth adoption had been accomplished. Mostly, however, I was afraid. "Does your therapist know about these plans?" she asked Amy accusingly. "Why don't you call her now and let's see what she says," she said more as a command than as an invitation. With every word, I felt as though Ms. Bitt was taking a bite out of me.

Amy dialed her therapist's number to tell her of her decision. Her therapist, who answered right away, was disbelieving. She insisted on speaking to me to confirm Amy's story. The room became smaller as I took the receiver. Amy's therapist interrogated me for several minutes before I put a stop to it. "Who are you?" she demanded to know. "Where are you? Is it true you want to adopt Amy's baby?" She sounded angry at me and at her client— inappropriately so I thought. What was going on here? Did they have more than a professional relationship? Why had she lost her professional distance? When I had enough, I simply said, "Well, I think I've answered your questions. Goodbye for now," and hung up the telephone.

The results of the testing showed that Amy's pelvis was too small to safely deliver vaginally. The baby was having trouble descending into the birth canal. The doctor recommended a C-section. They decided to admit her and do the operation that afternoon. Amy named me to be in the delivery room with her. The birth was going to come soon and I was becoming more anxious with each passing minute. Since there was going to be a waiting period of several hours, I excused myself to keep my appointments at work. Driving away from the hospital gave me the opportunity to ponder the enormity of what was about to happen. I was about to adopt a baby from a woman I believed was unstable, in a hospital where the social worker was hostile, and no one had been prepared by the attorneys. Worse, Amy's therapist was opposed and she apparently wielded great power over Amy. I called Sam and brought him up to speed on what was happening.

Later in the day, after seeing the last of my patients, I called

Amy at the hospital and learned that the operation had been postponed until the next morning. As she requested, I picked Amy up from the hospital and drove her back to the motel to pick up her car and personal belongings. Her short-term lease had expired and she could not go back because she had no money. She was homeless. Fortunately, we had a friend who owned a downtown hotel whom we pressed into service. He not only provided Amy with a suite, but with room service as well. So far, we had managed to clear each hurdle. I was relieved that we didn't have to put her up at our house.

Amy insisted on driving herself to the new hotel. She said that she had "some things to do" before she went there. I left her, against my better judgement, in the parking lot of her motel. It was nerve-wracking to consider that she was nine months pregnant and driving herself around Baltimore at night. At the hotel, I knew Amy would be treated like a queen. We parted with an agreement that we would pick her up at six thirty the next morning for the big event. My sleep that night was fitful.

Chapter Two

*I*t was January eighteenth—before dawn. The sky was dark at that early hour and it was cold out. Frozen snow lay on the ground in sooty piles. Sam and I pulled up to the hotel precisely at six thirty as promised. Amy was waiting in the lobby, suitcase in hand, looking scared, lonely and confused. I gently guided her to my car while Sam got her keys so that he could drive her car for her. Until she entered my car, she was silent. As we pulled away from the hotel, Amy started to speak incoherently. She told me that she and the baby were going to go to her therapist's home to live. Then she said she was not really pregnant and didn't want to have an operation. I became very frightened, thinking she was losing touch with reality. At that moment, in my opinion, she was incompetent to give legal consent for anything, let alone a Caesarian section or an adoption. With her ranting, the adoption seemed to be disintegrating before my eyes. I steeled my nerves for the half-hour drive to the hospital.

We arrived on time and Sam and I accompanied Amy to the labor area. We did our best to comfort her and calm her down while the nurse poked at her bloated arm repeatedly in unsuccessful attempts to find a vein. She finally had to call an intravenous therapist to do it. Throughout the morning, we stayed with Amy and tried to calm her as we waited for the surgery to begin. Sam had witnessed C-sections before, so Amy elected me to be with her in the operating room.

While we waited, we saw our obstetrician friend, Dr. Shelly, turn the corner of the labor and delivery area. He practically bumped into us. It was comforting to see his smiling, mustachioed face in such unfamiliar surroundings. Shelly had been two years ahead of Sam in his residency at this hospital. He gave us a hug and offered us words of encouragement and support before he continued on his rounds. That Sam had trained at this hospital, even that he knew some of the nurses and they knew him, was of little comfort to me. I felt like an intruder, someone there to take someone else's baby away. Ordinary adoptive parents are out of place in a hospital where someone else is having their baby. We felt extraordinarily awkward.

At eight forty-five a.m., my world began to cave in. Amy's therapist swept into the labor area and ushered us out so she could consult with her client privately. We told her we would be in the waiting room so that she would know where to find me when it was time to prep for the surgery. Stupid me. Saying "See you later" while she greeted her therapist was the last time I ever spoke to Amy.

Sam and I went to the waiting room, expecting that I'd be called at any moment to witness the delivery. With each passing minute, my heart sank as it became increasingly apparent that they had started without me. After three hours of waiting, I knew the baby must already be born. I had missed the birth. Very likely, the adoption had already aborted.

At noon, Amy's therapist came out to see us. She told us that Amy had delivered a healthy baby but she wouldn't tell us whether it was a boy or a girl. She said Amy had changed her mind about having me in the operating room, opting instead to have her therapist witness the delivery. She also said that Amy had asked her therapist to make all decisions for her. We were stunned and confused. She said we could see neither Amy nor the baby. She was severe and terse, barely making eye contact with either of us. She indicated nothing about the condition of the mother or the baby. She refused to explain any of the circumstances of Amy's wishes or to answer any of our questions. I had the impression that she took some private satisfaction at being the messenger with such bad news.

After our short meeting, we had nothing to do but go home empty-handed. Before leaving the hospital, we sent Amy a bouquet of flowers, had a telephone installed in her room, left a note reiterating our interest in adoption and called our attorney with the devastating news. Amy's reversal had the same effect on me as if the child—my child—had died.

On the way home, I tried to fit the pieces of this puzzle together. In my grief, I railed against Amy. She was stuck: no money, no home, and no boyfriend to take care of her. Unwilling to approach her relatives, she hit on unwitting victims, easy marks: doctors, homosexuals (who cared about them anyway?), do-gooders, patsies. Amy had exploited our kindness and our desperate need to have a family to see her through a crisis. She pretended all that she said—everything she knew we wanted to hear—in order to get what she wanted from us: to be taken care of in a crisis. "This is your baby. I'm just providing it with a safe haven until it is born and I can give it to you....." Her hollow words echoed in my mind—all fraud.

The next day, Saturday, Amy's attorney visited her client in her hospital room. Amy was feeding the baby when she came in. Amy's therapist insisted on the baby rooming in with her. Amy's attorney told her that Sam and I had to know by the next day if she was going to go through with the adoption or not, even though I had already given up hope.

On Sunday, Sam called Amy and asked to see her. He wanted to personally reaffirm our commitment to adopt if Amy didn't want the baby. I was too hurt to go along. I didn't think I could bear to see the baby. Amy assented and Sam drove in by himself. When he entered her room, he saw the bassinet by Amy's bedside. In it was a gorgeous, healthy, ten pound baby boy. He told me later that he wanted to snatch that baby up and whisk it away to safety, but all he could do was hold him for a minute to say goodbye. Amy was ambivalent and confused about her ability and desire to parent her child. Earlier, she had asked her attorney to come in with the relinquishment forms to sign. Later, she threw her out.

By the end of the day, we were exhausted. Sam returned home feeling as I did: used up, profoundly saddened, and angry. More than anything, we were terrified for the baby. In a conversation with her obstetrician that night, we learned that she, too, was saddened by the turn of events and concerned for the baby. There was nothing anyone could do about it.

In the days and weeks that followed, I remained depressed, withdrawn, and bitter. I had never experienced such profound emptiness in my life. I was angry at the lawyers, to whom we had paid thousands of dollars. I was furious with Amy's therapist, who acted like a jealous lover and treated us as shabbily as had her patient. The frustration of not being able to do anything about it was unbearable. It would take months for me to realize that I could transform the pain of this loss into emotional fuel to conduct a search for our child. It was too early to know that this search would become the most consuming passion I ever felt and that I would not rest until I found my child. Out of my grief grew my resolve. As the weeks passed, I realized more than ever that this aching in my guts was not just mourning for a lost child, but the most intense desire I had ever felt to have a baby of my own.

At forty years of age, the threshold of mid-life, I seemed to have everything anyone could want: a devoted lover of fourteen years, a beautiful home, a fascinating, well-paying job, a position in the community, loving, caring friends, some going back thirty years, and, most importantly, wonderful family relations on both sides of our families. Yet, despite this, I felt incomplete.

By March, I realized that this aching would never go away until we had a child. This was when the real healing began. I didn't care if it was a son or daughter, if the baby was biologically related or not. I resolved that I would not rest until we had a baby and created our own family. Intuitively, I felt that our first child would be a boy. When I began writing to him in my journal before he came, I used "Simon," a strong name with biblical roots. Sam and I chose that name together—it was the only name in our baby-naming book we both liked. If it was a girl, her first name would be Gloria in memory of my mother. Her middle name would be Fay in memory of Sam's grandmother and in honor of my grandmother, both of whom shared the same name.

I had no way of explaining this insistent inner demand for a child. One friend suggested that I was entering a mid-life crisis; another, that perhaps something was going wrong with my relationship with Sam. A third wondered if I wanted "old-age insurance." Yet another wondered if I just wanted to make a political statement.

Can any prospective parent know all the complex reasons why

he or she wants a child? I'm sure it's far more than biology—the fact that they have the organs do it. When I asked myself this question, I couldn't answer it with certainty. Ever since I became aware of the possibility that we could have a child by alternative means, I felt that something was missing from our life that only a baby could complete. First and foremost, I was aware of simply yearning to have a family. To me, a family meant two parents (whatever their gender) and two children, just like the one in which I had been raised. Raising children would add more meaning to my life.

But perhaps the unusual brand of emptiness I felt was for other reasons beyond my conscious desire to raise kids. Maybe, as one friend suggested, I wanted a baby just because society said I shouldn't have one. I knew I was angry with myself for buying that message earlier in life. Maybe a part of it was the surfacing of some latent desire to continue the family name, create an heir and pass on the benefits of my knowledge, experience, and worldly possessions. Could I have wanted a baby so badly just so I could bolster my position as a gay role model? Can anyone's reasons to procreate be free of selfish motives? I finally decided that I couldn't know every component in this decision. After we lost Amy's baby, I would not, could not rest until we had a child. Sam was with me on this, although his need was unspoken. He articulated this desire to have a child in his quiet but strong support of me.

I was reminded of the expression, "If life serves you lemons, make lemonade." Well, I'd had some lemons in my life. My father died when I was seventeen. My mother, an author and social worker known for her work with families of gay people, died suddenly when I was thirty-four and now we had lost this baby. We'd lost more friends to AIDS than I cared to count and we were still counting. If those weren't lemons, I didn't know what was. The lemonade I was about to make was to get a job. This job would be full-time and it's description would be simple: Get a baby.

Chapter Three

Two months after the Amy debacle, I had sufficiently recovered to make a resolution. I was determined to do something every day to take us closer to our goal of having a baby. I spoke with people in adoption circles to find out how to get a baby. I read every book I could find in the library on the subject. Among other things, I learned early on that if I presented myself as part of a gay couple, I'd kill our chances of adopting. Even though single parent adoptions are legal everywhere, there is discrimination against men. Over 95% of single parent adoptions are accomplished by women. One social worker told me that in her agency there had been only half a dozen adoptions in the last decade for single men. In her office if a single man were known to be gay, he would be eliminated as a candidate. As if these prejudices weren't enough, I also had to contend with being forty, the magic cut-off age for many adoption agencies. It looked more and more as though independent adoption would be the route for us. But where would we find a pregnant woman who would give up her baby to two gay men?

Everything about our lives which made us outstanding candidates to adopt seemed to be overshadowed by our sexual orientation. I hated that. Something that was such an insignificant part of what made a good parent seemed to count for so much in the adoption field. We were loving, bright, nurturing people. We knew how to parent, were well-off by most standards and could offer a child a wealth of experiences. We had a large home with plenty of room for kids. We valued education and we had excellent problem-solving skills. We had a substantial circle of loving family and friends—all of whom were rooting for us. If Sam or I were a woman, agencies and individuals would consider us ideal candidates.

Despite my recovery, the crisis of January still haunted me. It was hard to see a baby or hear parents talk of their children without thinking of our loss—and Simon. I never knew a man could ache so for a child. I thought only women had biological clocks. I wanted a child to hold and protect and love. I wanted to nourish and guide, to give a good life to this child. I wanted to help him grow to realize his full potential, unhampered by psychological problems. I knew I could do this. I was confident in Sam and I was confident in us as a couple.

I often thought of my mother when I thought of parenting. I wanted to pass along the love she gave to me; the private, happy times of childhood: trips to the movies or to visit sights like the Empire State Building, shopping, scouting, summer camp. Loving and raising a child would be a fitting memorial to both my parents. They valued family life, as did Sam and I. They sacrificed much to give my brother and me a good life. This journey to Simon stimulated a great deal of reflection about my own life.

When I was a little boy in Forest Hills, New York, I spent my first seven years sharing a bedroom with my older brother while my parents slept on a convertible sofa in the living room of our one-bedroom apartment. I remembered my mother, who treated me so specially, and my father, who seemed so proud of me—he used to call me his "golden child." Simon would have more privileges than I had as a child—certainly more room. But he could not have more love and support.

My father, who changed his name from Siegfried Morgenroth to Fred Morgen, was a tall, thin Austrian immigrant who came with his family to the United States in the early 30's, just before the Holocaust. He spoke with a strong accent (we used to joke that he couldn't even pronounce my mother's name correctly: "Gloya" he used to call her). He had traditional family values and an authoritarian style. In his world, children were respectful, obedient, and supposed to be seen, not heard. Though successful in business, he regretted not having a college education. Like so many immigrants, he wanted a better life for his children and encouraged us in academics. He made it no secret that he wanted us to be doctors, a profession he deified.

My father owned his own importing business and worked very hard, sometimes traveling as far away as Japan to conduct trade. As a child, I occasionally accompanied my father to work on Saturdays, went with him on business trips and took orders for him at the many trade shows he attended. He always gave me something to do which made me feel worthwhile. He loved me a great deal and, as with my mother, was openly affectionate with me. I was heartbroken when he died of leukemia just before I graduated high school.

My mother, Gloria Guss Back—twelve years younger than my father—was the pampered, first-generation American daughter of a Latvian leather merchant. She was a beautiful woman with dark hair and eyes, smooth, clear skin, a shapely figure, and a wonderful sense of humor. She loved to joke and prided herself on her sense of the ridiculous. Whereas my father taught me how to work, my mother taught me how to laugh. Later in life, after she remarried when I was a junior in college, Mom went back to school to finish the college education she had started thirty years before. Hungry for knowledge, she didn't stop until she got her master's degree in social work, became an accomplished educator and group leader, and distinguished herself by writing a widely read book for the families of gay people entitled *ARE YOU STILL MY MOTHER, Are you Still My Family?* (Warner, 1985). I'm still proud of her for her acccomplishments.

My parents married young and started their family right away. My brother was a "war baby," born two years after the end of World War II. Life in my family was quite traditional. Mom stayed at home and took care of the children. Dad went to work.

From the time I was seven years old until I was fourteen, my mother worked summers at a summer camp in exchange for our attending that camp for eight weeks. My father visited on alternate weekends. I was proud that my mother, the "camp mother" was popular with the other campers and the counselors alike.

It was in this camp that I first became aware that I was different from the other boys. I secretly had crushes on one counselor or another throughout the years I attended. I admired their bodies and knew it was more than just wanting to emulate them that made me so interested. I wanted to touch them and be touched by them. I didn't know the words to explain my attraction. My ever-growing awareness of these feelings throughout childhood and adolescence and into adulthood was a source of both my greatest pleasure and most persistent fear. Without ever being told, I knew that the feelings I had discovered were taboo—I just didn't know why. As with many gay kids, I always thought I was the only one—that there was nobody else who felt these same forbidden feelings. I was constantly concerned about being discovered.

Early in life, I admired the muscle builders pictured on the backs of comic books. The compelling sexual attraction to their physiques was undeniable. Later, I remember receiving a book when I turned thirteen and celebrated my bar mitzvah—a pictorial essay of Michelangelo's work. How I fell in love with his David. Throughout my adolescence, he fueled my most intense sexual fantasies.

In my junior high and high school years, I started experimenting with my best friend, Hank. We would go to his house after school and practice giving each other back rubs. These massages eventually led to more intimate touching. We never spoke about what we were doing, nor did we label it. If one of our mothers came home while we were pleasuring each other, we were lightening-quick in zipping up and pretending we were watching television. I remember one afternoon in particular, when I was about twelve. Mrs. Kernan came home and exclaimed, "Hank...your face is so red, what have you been doing? Do you have a fever?" Trembling with fear and excitement, we dared not reveal why we were both so hot. I fled in terror. I learned on my own that such feelings and actions were not to be discussed with anyone—even the person you were doing it with.

Despite the persistence of my homoerotic fantasies throughout high school, I also found myself attracted to girls. Whatever sexual confusion I suffered throughout my adolescence, I developed genuine feelings of affection and attraction for the various girlfriends I dated until I graduated from college. In my second year of college, it had become the "Age of Aquarius" and bisexuality was "in." I felt part of an elite as I alternated dates between my boyfriend and my girlfriend at New York University in Greenwich Village.

For many non-gay people, it is difficult to comprehend how one's awareness of a homosexual orientation develops. For gay people, it is the easiest thing in the world to understand. Integrating those different perspectives comprises some of what I do professionally when I am called upon to counsel gay people and their families. I explain that a gay person's awareness of their homosexual orientation begins just the same as that of their heterosexual counterparts: as a gradual discovery. People don't choose to be gay any more than they choose to be right-handed. The feelings just gradually emerge into consciousness. Sometimes the process can take decades.

It wasn't until I was well into adulthood that I identified myself as gay; in college I considered myself bisexual. What I now know as really perverted in me was thinking that as long as I dated women as well as men, I would never be completely gay, something that I felt was anathema. It took a long time to develop a positive gay identity, something I'm grateful I now have. It's a challenge for young gay men and lesbians to develop a positive self-image when they learn that their feelings are "forbidden" from such an early age.

When I was a teenager, I used to wonder how I could be gay and have a family. I thought that my gayness was something I'd grow out of when I graduated from high school, that I'd somehow shed it magically, like molting. I never dreamed that I'd wind up getting married to another man. I fully expected to have a wife and children and family life just as my parents did. Considering, however, my professional and personal aspirations—college, graduate school, international travel, a home, property—I expected that my family would come after I settled down—at least not before I turned thirty. Because this was so many years away from the days of my young adulthood, with so many distractions along the way, the thought of children was compartmentalized into a small space in the rear of my mind, only to be reviewed when I was reminded of children, for example at the births of my contemporaries' children.

Although I dated both men and women in college, it wasn't until I was in graduate school that I first fell in love with a man. The infatuation I felt for Alexander was profound and unmatched in my previous experience. After an appropriate courtship, we began living together. I fully expected to spend the rest of my life with him. Some relationships don't turn out the way you expect, however. We separated after three years. I was distraught when it ended. I even reverted to dating women. At the age of twenty-six, I was confused again.

Sad over losing Alexander, bored with my job counseling alcoholics for the county, and hungry for more life experience, I rented out my home and took a year off to travel abroad. I applied to doctoral programs in psychology before I left and was accepted at a professional school in San Diego. It was there that I worked and studied harder than I ever had in my life to earn my Ph.D. It was toward the end of my first year that I met Sam, the man with whom I would be destined to spend the rest of my life.

My lover Sam is 5'9", trim, and ruggedly attractive. Despite his smooth skin and boyish physique, he has the face of someone older than his years—as if the lines reflect the pain he attempts to relieve for the many terminally ill patients he attends. His eyes are hazel and he is clean-shaven. He smiles charmingly and often and inspires confidence and affection in all who know him. He loves to laugh and plays bridge with a passion that borders on obsession. A responder rather than an initiator like me, Sam accepts life as it comes rather than trying to change it. Sam is also a procrastinator—something I attribute to his coming from California. But his procrastination helps him to focus his attention on the thing he does best: doctoring. Sam's reputation in our community is akin to a gay Marcus Welby, M.D. Everyone who knows him professionally as well as personally loves his compassionate style, his easygoing nature, and generosity with his time. I'm proud of the scrapbooks of "thank you" notes Sam has accumulated over the years. This man loves and nurtures me quietly, reliably, and completely.

One great source of pleasure for Sam has nothing to do with medicine. Reflective of his nurturing nature, Sam is a culinary genius. His renewal each day comes from concocting and assembling dishes, creating sauces, coordinating colors and tastes on the plate and seeing others enjoy his efforts. Needless to say, our friends and family love his cooking and I am his greatest fan. If only his dishes had fewer calories (or his lover had greater self-control).

Sam was the second of four children born to a transplanted educator father from Kansas and an elementary school teacher mother from a small inland town in southern California. The family was a close one, with five years separating the first two and last two children. Throughout his childhood, Sam recalls other children staying with his family in addition to his siblings, whether they were cousins from homes less fortunate than Sam's or exchange students. Because of this, it always seemed as if he had at least four siblings rather than three. Sam's grandfather was the postmaster of the town in which he grew up. That, coupled with his parents' positions in the school system—his father was the principal of the only junior high school in town—demanded exemplary behavior from Sam, something he always managed to attain.

Sam was always fascinated with nature and recalls fondly how his father would bring home educational movies from school to show the children at home. The family raised fruits and vegetables in their garden and animals for 4-H. Sam enjoyed talking about his pig, Cleopatra, which won an award one year. One of my favorite photographs of Sam was a close-up taken on a boat while on a scuba-diving vacation in the Caribbean. He was inspecting a sea snail perched on his forefinger like a parakeet inches from his face. It seemed to capture his delight in nature and his love of all forms of life.

Like me, Sam had always been aware of his feelings of attraction to men. Without role models, however, he never dared to express those feelings until he went away to college. Also like me, Sam had a girlfriend in high school. Despite genuine feelings of affection for Lissie which persist to this day, Sam fought his nature until he found himself in college. It wasn't until then that he was finally ready to come out to his family. He chose his father, first, who responded with equanimity, saying that he was still his son and he would always love him. He exhorted him not to tell his mother, fearing the news would hurt her too much. Several years passed before he found the courage to tell his mother. Happily, she, too, responded well, despite deeply entrenched religious beliefs which taught her that homosexuality was sinful.

One of the most important experiences in Sam's life which helped him to define himself as a person and gave him a broader perspective on the world was his two years of international travel. Right out of high school, never having been away from home for more than a few days, Sam spent one year in Sweden as an exchange student. Living with a family from another culture, especially the aristocratic family he was placed with, enriched his life, his ability for language, and his understanding of people immeasurably. Before he entered medical school, he again had the opportunity to go abroad—this time to France, where he taught and traveled for a year.

Sam had just finished his second year of medical school when we met at a party. He was nothing like my type (nor was I like his I later learned). Whereas I liked swarthy Mediterraneans, Sam was smooth and fair. It didn't take long to rediscover that we fall in love with people, not types. We weren't introduced at the party until it was time to leave, but something about his smile and our handshake foretold that something significant was about to occur in my life. After saying "Hello," we exchanged meaningful looks and arranged to meet the next day. Our afternoon date turned into dinner, which turned into breakfast the following morning. The more time we spent together, the more we discovered we had in common. We were both fluent in French, loved international travel, had doctoral ambitions, were comfortable with our gay identities, including being "out" to our families, and had a similar sense of humor. In the weeks that followed what turned out to be a three-day date, I fell in love with Sam and he with me. As the weeks turned into months, I had a growing confidence that this would be the man with whom I would spend the rest of my life.

Because we both had previous significant relationships that had soured, we decided to undertake pre-marital counseling prior to moving in together. This was an excellent way to explore our expectations of the relationship. A skilled therapist assisted us in achieving a mutual understanding about what being married to another man would mean. In the many years since those sessions, I have often reflected on the things we talked about and feel grateful that we solved many of our potential problems before they ever came up.

We had a fifteen month courtship before we decided to live together. In September, we began our new life together as a couple in a large, old, light-filled apartment with a balcony overlooking San Diego's gorgeous Balboa Park. Our honeymoon year together was the happiest of my life. That same year I completed my doctoral training and began a one year postdoctoral psychology internship. Sam was to complete medical school one year later. Our future together looked rosy.

Before Sam applied to residency programs, we had extensive discussions about where we wanted to live and work after graduate school. Because medical students were selected for residencies through a computerized matching program, he was not entirely in control of that decision. Ultimately, he selected and was selected by a family practice training program in Baltimore. He left for Baltimore in July and I followed at the end of my internship the following September. We were sad to leave southern California. I was so reluctant to leave that I even missed my plane!

As we grew together as a couple, our lives followed a rather predictable course. We bought a beautiful piece of secluded, wooded land, tore down the old house that was on it, built a home on the old foundation, and developed a circle of friends whom we now consider our family. The early years in Maryland were hard. Sam worked 140 hour weeks as an intern and then a resident and, having finished my pre- and post-doctoral internships the year before, I worked hard at getting licensed and building a private practice.

Our early years in Maryland were also characterized by extensive public service. Sam became the medical director for a gay and lesbian outpatient clinic; I founded the local gay and lesbian business and professional association and was active in the state psychological association in the area of gay concerns. We both became involved early on in a study to help the AIDS research effort at Johns Hopkins. As the epidemic took on more grisly proportions, all we could think was, "There but for the grace of God, go I." Many of our friends succumbed and it became a painful ritual each year to delete names from our address books.

As time passed, Sam's family practice became largely gay and disproportionately weighted with patients living with HIV disease. As my practice became more established, I, too, had a larger than average number of gay and lesbian clients. Because of my interest in the subject, I took leadership positions in professional as well as political gay-related activities. In addition to spearheading a drive to pass an equal rights amendment for gays and lesbians in Baltimore County, an effort which is being reenacted in jurisdictions around the country, I conducted research into homophobic violence.

In those early years, despite my adolescent projections about building a family later in life, having children seemed premature. I had always thought it would happen eventually, but I wanted to complete our nest first, a job which never seemed to get finished. I wanted to accumulate savings and allow time for both of us to establish our practices. I wanted vacations for us. We always put off into the future the time we would try for a baby. When I did think about it, it seemed a huge and difficult undertaking. How do two men have a baby together anyway? They never taught us that one in psychology classes or medical school. Imagine my surprise when Sam brought home Amy's letter that June. I was four months shy of forty and Sam was almost thirty-eight. We were as ready as we ever were going to be. But the dream-come true turned into a nightmare.

Chapter Four

*I*n the first month of my new job of finding a baby, work was going well. I found myself on the phone a lot: amending ads, leaving messages for people, fielding rejections, and returning from dead ends. I wrote to lawyers, obstetricians, midwives, adoption agencies, anyone I could think of who might be able to help us find a baby.

To broaden the range of possibilities, I decided not to limit our search to adoption. I began considering using a surrogate mother. To that end, I read everything I could get my hands on about surrogacy and spoke with numerous agencies and professionals around the country who ran surrogate mother programs. I ordered adoption and surrogacy manuals and placed ads in all the major East Coast gay newspapers, mistakenly thinking that the only woman who would be sympathetic to a gay male couple and who might consider having a baby for them would be a lesbian. I even placed advertisements for both an adoption and a surrogate mother in a state-wide advertising throwaway, the *Pennysaver*:

SURROGATE MOTHER WANTED: Loving, professional couple will pay fee for services rendered. Completely legal. {telephone}

The more I thought about it, the more surrogacy appeared to be a lesser risk than adoption. If a snafu occurred, at least we'd be entitled to custody because of our biological relationship with the child. On the other hand, if a surrogacy were disputed, we could be held legally responsible for providing child support for eighteen years with the likelihood that we'd never get custody if we tried to fight for it in court. That possibility terrified me.

While I became ever more involved in the search, Sam indicated that he didn't want to get so caught up in this baby business that that would be all we'd ever talk about. I was sarcastic in my reply, hurt that he was already complaining about the journey when the train was just leaving the station and angry that he seemed to be anticipating failure. Out of that discussion, however, came an agreement that each of us would do at least one thing every day to take us closer to our goal. That could be as easy as telling someone new that we were looking for a baby. As our journey got started, everyone I spoke to—family, friends, even strangers—encouraged us to keep up with our efforts.

One question was whether to advertise in straight publications. By doing so, I was afraid we would face multiple disappointments when the women found out we were gay. On the other hand, those were the publications that women most likely to have children read. Should we stick with the gay publications or take the risk? If only there were directions we could follow. We had to figure everything out on our own...just as with the rest of our lives as gay people.

By mid-March, we took another positive step. We went to our first meeting of the Association of Single Adoptive Parents. The evening's talk was entitled, "Telling the Adoption Story," and it was to be conducted by an adoptive mother of three "international" children. Sam and I were encouraged and it marked the first time I really began to think we could make this happen.

The meeting was in a church in downtown Washington, D.C. When we entered the downstairs meeting hall, most people were already seated in a loose circle. Before the invited speaker took the floor, a thirty-something single man gave us an introduction to single parent adoption. His success in finding two children gave us encouragement that we, too, could get a baby. When he went around the room and asked each of us to describe ourselves and tell why we had come and where we were in the adoptive process, I breathed a sigh of relief that he was going counter-clockwise. Sam was sitting to my left. I hated facing the decision of whether or not to come out to a group of strangers. It never ceases to amaze me how something that is so natural, so typical for heterosexual couples—introducing a spouse—is an act of courage for gay and lesbian couples. When it came Sam's turn to speak, he said he was just starting the investigation process and was there to learn and get information about adoption. I was surprised and hurt by his failure to mention that he was really a we and that it was we who were seeking to adopt. Coming out as a couple was up to me.

When my turn came, I was afraid that coming out might jeopardize our chances to get a baby, even though this was a support group, not an adoption agency. Yet I knew that trying to pass as straight men might have worse consequences. After a pause, I introduced myself as Sam's partner and indicated that we had been a couple for over ten years. Happily, we were welcomed warmly. Most of the advice we got that evening was that we should not come out during the adoption process. "You either want a baby or you want to make a political statement," we were told emphatically. However much that advice conflicted with my values, the stakes were too high for me to take a chance on losing Simon before we ever got him home. I never forgot those words. I later learned that four out of five men in the group that night were PLU's.

The invited speaker spoke for an hour and a half on the developmental stages of adoptive childhood and what to expect from adopted children. She humanized her talk by telling funny anecdotes about her own mixed German, English, Greek, and Korean family. It was inspiring to hear how two parents assimilated international babies into their lives and respected the cultures from which the babies had come. The speaker suggested a great idea: write a letter to our baby before he comes, keep it, and maybe show it to him when he's older and going through adolescent rebellion or some other developmental/psychological problem. It resonated in me as I had so much to express. My letter would tell our baby how much we loved him and wanted him and how hard we were working to get him. As time passed, I would write many letters to our unborn Simon.

When we arrived home that night, we received calls from two of the men at the meeting, each coming out to us and each providing us with helpful information. This reaffirmed my belief that gay people belong to a vast international fraternity. When we recognize each other, no matter where in the world we are, we go out of our way to help—and kibbutz with—each other.

The trip home flew by; we had so much to discuss. While Sam juggled the steering wheel and the car phone, talking simultaneously with a patient in the hospital and me, I started writing an agenda from ideas generated by the meeting. One of the things I was learning about this business of searching for a baby was that I had to regard it as at least a part-time job. Like anything that was worth doing, it required two to four hours per day. Almost an hour later, I had generated a list of things to do that would take at least a day to complete.

The more I worked, the more fascinating I found the intricacies of adoption. Despite this, I remained haunted by the surrogate mother option. It was hard to deny the part of me that wanted a biologically-related baby even though I knew that I would love any baby I adopted. I saw a crossroads coming—forcing a choice I didn't want to have to make. Surrogacy? Adoption? Each had its own risks, merits, and complications.

In my search, I considered a "special needs" child. This was a euphemism for a child with emotional or physical deficits. God, how I feared that term. I didn't know if I could raise a child knowing in advance the challenges we'd face. We had decided that if a child of one of us born to a surrogate mother had special needs, we would take care of him unflinchingly as best we could. However, after much soul searching and discussion, Sam and I decided we would not adopt such a child.

The day after our Association of Single Adoptive Parents meeting, I got a third call from another member of the group. He gave me the number of a past member who he thought might be able to help Sam and me. Sam predicted he, too, would be gay. The first thing out of his mouth was that he was a gay father of two! We talked for an hour about his adoption experiences. Articulate, interesting, helpful, he sensed exactly where we were in our journey and offered many helpful hints. He drew our attention to the advantages of

Chilean or other South American adoption sources. Was Simon going to be South American? Time would tell.

Chapter Five

*A*t the end of March, two months after we lost Amy's baby, we received our first response to our advertising. The voice on the answering machine, soft and tentative, said, "My name is Tara Miller. I'm calling about your ad in the *Pennysaver*." I called Sam immediately to share the exciting news. We had a prospective surrogate mother!

I called Tara back and talked with her at length. Tara was twenty-three and lived in a small southern Maryland town with her husband, two toddlers, a roommate and her roommate's child in a home owned by her in-laws. A full-time homemaker, she told me she loved being pregnant, but had her hands full with the three children in the home. Her husband, an apprentice plumber, definitely did not want more children. She started to say she thought she might like more, then her voice trailed off. She said she didn't have the patience for more but she missed being pregnant. She felt the need for a purpose in life, to make a unique contribution—to do something on her own in addition to caring for her family. She said, "This is something I can do." She was sure she could give up a baby after carrying it for nine months, but she said her husband was against the idea when she brought it up at dinner. Although unspoken, I sensed that her family could use the money and carrying a baby for someone else would be a job at which she could earn money that wouldn't interfere with her domestic responsibilities.

In our phone conversation, I spelled out everything I knew

about surrogacy from the books and the medical and legal journal articles I had read. I was balanced in my approach, explaining the pros and cons of surrogacy for both the birthmother and the biological father. I told her that, up until January, I hadn't really known any more about surrogacy than the average person. What I did know, I had learned from the notorious Baby M case. I further explained that from my reading, I learned that it was actually happening all around the country. I told her how much I had learned from reading, and suggested some titles that were in the library so she could acquaint herself with the subject. I suggested reading a book by an actual surrogate mother which might help her to decide if she could or really wanted to do it. As we ended our conversation, Tara said not to get our hopes up, that she wasn't making any commitments, but that she was curious and wanted more information.

I was relieved and yet apprehensive that my homosexuality or my relationship with Sam had not come up. I guessed Tara was so preoccupied with how the experience would affect her that she couldn't yet think about the person who would be inseminating her. I told her about our two disappointments with adoption and how desperate we were to have children. I told her that we were considering surrogacy as a last chance, and that I would also copy some articles on the subject and send them to her. I knew we were going to have to disclose the nature of our relationship but I didn't know when or how. If the down sides of surrogacy weren't enough, our homosexuality might send this couple running. I included some letters of reference as a precaution.

Damn. How I hated homophobia. I knew it was based on ignorance and fear. I resented constantly having to educate so many of people with whom I came in contact. Being gay was about as relevant to anything (except babymaking) as being left-handed. I knew the best way to proceed was to develop a relationship with an individual or couple first, let them get to know me as a person, and then somehow introduce them to the concept that our committed gay relationship was exactly the same as a heterosexual marriage except in the eyes of the law. I didn't know how I was going to come out to this person. We signed off agreeing that she was going to read up on the subject, talk more to her husband, and call me collect the next time she was ready to talk.

Now that we had found a prospective candidate, I had even more homework to do. I needed to research the law pertaining to adoption and surrogacy in Maryland, while continuing the surrogate mother and adoption searches in case Tara didn't work out. Sam said we should re-run our ad in the *Pennysaver*, considering how quickly we got a response from it. I did this as well as putting an ad in the local Sunday paper.

The evening Tara called, Sam and I again discussed the importance of having a biological connection with the baby. Sam did not feel the need to have his own genes carried on. I was not so sure. I really couldn't explain it. I knew there were children in this world waiting to be adopted...children already here. Why would I want to bring another one into the world? Just how strong was this tug for a biological connection? However a child came to us, we intended to make a life-long commitment, to nurture that child to adulthood: to teach him, love him, care for him, protect him, prepare him for a good life. By adoption or through a surrogate mother, all I really wanted was a baby.

If we were going to use a surrogate mother, who would be the father? How would we decide? It was at this time that the idea of creating a "milkshake" came into being. Not only did this seem fair, but, more romantically, it came closest to the ideal of making our own baby. Hopefully, we would find a birthmother who would appreciate and cooperate with our plan. As the speaker at the Association of Single Adoptive Parents meeting had suggested, I wrote a letter to Simon with the hope that our son would read it one day.

March 20

Dear Simon,

I don't know when we will see each other but I hope and I pray it's soon. I know you can read my heart and feel my love. You know how much I have to give you. Please, stay strong. Dad is coming closer to you every day. I know you're drifting closer to me every day. What does

it feel like? Are you happy? Are you preparing for your
arrival? Prayerfully soon we will be together forever.
I will never lose faith that will happen. Somehow, I feel
certain that you're going to be in my arms by next
March. Maybe you'll be born on your grandma's
birthday, March 4. I'll write you again.

Love Dad

It was then that I realized that Sam and I needed to decide what the baby would call each of us. With two fathers, we couldn't both be "Dad." That night, Sam and I had a lengthy conversation about how we would have Simon address us. After considering the many alternatives, we arrived at "Dad" and "Daddy." I was to be "Dad" because that was what I called my father and it felt more comfortable for me. Sam was to be "Daddy" because that is what he called his father and it felt more comfortable for him. The discussion reminded me yet again how few role models gay people have and how we must constantly invent solutions that heterosexuals take for granted. For example, all of our verbal agreements needed to be recorded in notarized documents. We had wills, powers of attorney, a co-parenting agreement, and other documents necessary to establish our child's relationship with each of us, waiting to be signed once the child was born and the legal petitions were granted. We had to create documents addressing our family's needs, documents which married couples don't need because those relationships are prescribed and protected by law.

Simon's names for us also raised the question of what would be our roles. Sam and I had discussed this many times in the past and we knew that each of us wanted to be the mothering one as well as the father. We decided that ours would be a co-parenting arrangement where we would fully share all of the traditional child rearing responsibilities. Even though we could afford one, we would not hire a nanny. Neither of us was raised by a nanny and we weren't working this hard to have a child in order to have someone else raise him. We would adjust our schedules when the baby came so that I would be with him when Sam was at work and Sam would be with him when I was at work. We called this our "tag team" approach.

The night of Tara Miller's call, a second caller left a message. It was from Louise, a lesbian we knew to be an activist in the community who had heard through the grapevine that we were looking for a "woman's service." Louise invited us to call that evening. Imagine, two calls in one day! I thought this process would be like looking for a needle in a haystack. Now, we had options.

Each prospect had her advantages and disadvantages. The married woman with children had already borne children and knew what to expect. She was in a better position to prepare for relinquishment and give informed consent. A woman who'd never been pregnant couldn't possibly know how she'd feel after giving birth. Moreover, an older lesbian might feel this would be her one and only shot at having a child. Being independent, Louise would be financially able to raise a baby. On the other hand, if she changed her mind about relinquishing the baby, a court battle with her would be on a more equal footing than if a gay couple were suing a straight, married woman. Unbeknownst to us at the time, we would never hear from Tara Miller again.

Some gays and lesbians who were single opted for a "co-parenting" arrangement—that is, the biological parents would raise the child part-time in one parent's home, part-time in the other's, with the parents having joint custody. We were already clear we did not want such a co-parenting arrangement with a surrogate mother. We were so married, having our child's birthmother in his life with any authority would feel intrusive.

That night, I called Louise and invited her to come over the next Sunday. Knowing her to be sensitive to the politically correct, I was nervous that I might inadvertently do or say something to offend her. In our telephone conversation, she said she knew us as a couple by reputation and told me that she had always admired us. She revealed her colorful history, including a past marriage of convenience to a gay man. Apparently, she married this man to enable herself and her female lover at the time to become pregnant. Fortunately, she recalled in retrospect, she didn't become pregnant despite several tries and the three abandoned their efforts when the relationship with her female lover did not work out.

Bright and articulate, Louise now had a new lover, but they were still not quite sure of their commitment. She anticipated they would eventually want a child if their relationship became permanent. However, she was concerned about the health risks to both herself and her baby if she had her first child much later than now (she was thirty-four). She said she wanted to get pregnant now in order to confirm her fertility. Apparently, her unsuccessful efforts years earlier caused her to doubt her ability to conceive. Further, she anticipated a second pregnancy would be easier than the first so it would be better to have the more difficult pregnancy when she was younger and constitutionally better able to tolerate the attendant stresses—even if it meant having it for another couple. Her logic and motivation confused me despite her elaborate explanation.

Louise said that she would, in the future, be looking for a sperm donor. Interestingly, she implied that she might like one or both of us to be such donors. We decided to meet Sunday at our house and discuss things further. This would be our first face-to-face meeting with a surrogate mother candidate.

When Sunday came, I woke up early, a sure sign that I was anxious about protocol. What would Emily Post say? Do you raise the subject of sperm donation before noon at Sunday brunch? She would be coming to our house alone at 10:30. I had to clean house. Sam had to shop for brunch. He was relaxed enough to sleep until I woke him at 8:45.

How should I act? What should I say? Would we make small talk? Could we trust her? I developed a list of questions that Sam said made me look over-controlling. I tried to quell my nervousness by absorbing some of his calm.

While I was reading the newspaper before our meeting, an article about a proposed law outlawing surrogacy in Maryland commanded my attention. Senate Bill 322 passed the state Senate on March 15 and was forwarded to the House Judiciary Committee. If they passed it and the governor signed it, surrogate mother contracts would be banned as of July 1 the next year. This would mean an open window of opportunity only for just over a year. Would that be wide enough to have a baby by a surrogate before it became illegal? Weeks later I learned the bill had been defeated. What a relief it was to no longer have to contemplate the risk of running afoul of the law.

Louise arrived promptly at 10:30 neatly dressed in slacks and a suede vest. She was garrulous and talked at length about her involvement in the gay rights movement and told us her personal history, which involved many siblings and significant others. Unemployed at the time of our meeting, she had a good relationship with her family, who lived in the area. She believed most of her siblings would be supportive of her being a surrogate mother. Louise's family sounded healthy, non-addicted, long-lived, and without significant psychiatric illnesses. As with our first prospect, Tara, we compiled a long list of strengths and weaknesses afterwards. The only significant drawback was that Louise had never been pregnant.

Chapter Six

It was now the first day of spring. I was acutely aware of how much this season represents rebirth. Not since my grand obsessions of building our house or writing my doctoral dissertation had my energies been so productive. This was the second morning I'd awakened early. My mood was optimistic. I had renewed vigor and energy. I wasn't blue any more over the loss of Amy's baby, just frightened and excited. I was preparing to tackle this gargantuan undertaking—having a baby by a surrogate mother. For the time being I had put aside my pursuit of an independent adoption.

Since the calls from Tara and Louise, we had received three more calls from women interested in becoming surrogate mothers, all of them responding to our little ad in the *Pennysaver*. I couldn't believe our good fortune. We had found not only one woman to consider carrying our baby, but now a total of five. It amazed me that we might be able to pick and choose. Was our dream changing from a possibility to a probability?

That Friday, normally a day I took off, was proving to be quite hectic. I had agreed to take on a new patient who was in the hospital for severe depression and phobic anxiety. How could I function as a psychologist, patiently listening to peoples' problems, when so much was going on in my own life? I was reminded of the times of greatest crisis to me in the last decade—losing my mother and losing Amy's baby. I had been so profoundly sad. Yet I continued to function in my professional role. Sometimes, I wondered if I was expecting too much of myself. Shouldn't I have taken time off from work? Although the amount of stress I was under now was similar, the quality of that stress was different. I felt upbeat about what was happening, optimistic that we really were going to have a baby and that we were going to be a family. For the first time, I could even see this happening within the next year.

Before I went to see my patient in the hospital, I crafted a letter to Laura, candidate Number Three. We had shared much information in our two telephone conversations yesterday and the day before. Laura was thirty-three years old and married with three children. She had had two abortions. She had a miserable upbringing and seemed to be the kind of person I would more likely meet in my office as a patient than at my home as a friend. However, she was straight-forward and raised many interesting, legitimate questions. What would happen if the baby turned out to have some kind of serious medical problem? Did I expect one particular sex or another? Was this legal? What role would her husband play? Could he be there with her in the delivery room? How should she explain this to her two older children, ages ten and thirteen? How would it affect them? I answered her questions patiently, impressed with how this thoughtful abuse survivor and former runaway had turned her life around.

Before I set up a meeting with Laura in person, I told her I wanted to write her a letter. Sam and I agonized about the best way to do this, imagining different scenarios in which we told two strangers that we were a gay couple and that we wanted to have a baby. We were so afraid of rejection because of our sexual orientation. In two states, that discriminatory ignorance was even legislated by law, under the mistaken belief that merely being gay or lesbian implied unfitness for being a parent. Despite the risk of rejection, Sam and I had been steadfast in our belief that our relationship was our biggest asset. It was because of, not in spite of, that relationship that it would be in any child's interest to place him in our home. To try to ignore that would be like overlooking a married couple's relationship as a major strength in contributing to the well-being of their baby. I wrote, Sam reviewed, and off the letter went. We had now dubbed the letter written to surrogate candidate Number One, "The Letter." It was refined and reworked in the word processor and went out fresh to every new candidate. The Letter off, I was free to attend to my other responsibilities: testing at the hospital, two new patients in the office, assisting in a crisis between a gay father and his son who had just found out that the father was HIV positive.

By the time I got home, it was six o'clock. As I retrieved my messages from the machine, I was dumbfounded to hear the voice of a sixth prospective surrogate mother. I returned Catherine's call that evening. I told her a little about us, careful not to mention our genders. I asked her to tell me a bit about herself. All of five minutes passed before she told me that she was a lesbian! "I hope that doesn't disqualify me," she said shyly. I exclaimed my immediate relief and told her, "That's great! We're gay, too!"

This discovery led to further conversation about who we were, which then led to the realization that I had guest-lectured at her university class years before. Not only did she remember me, but she knew Sam by reputation. The more we talked, the safer we both felt. Talking to Catherine felt like coming home. Maybe she would be the one.

Catherine worked for an agency very close to our home that took care of disabled women. She was 25, a college graduate, single, and living with her sister. We arranged a personal meeting for the following Wednesday. I hung up feeling excited and impatient for Wednesday to come.

I couldn't believe the response we'd received from that little *Pennysaver* ad. We had an embarrassment of riches. A mere five days earlier we had been desolate, fearing that by going the adoption route, the process would take forever, drain us emotionally, and offer no guarantee that we would find an agency which would work with us, let alone a waiting child. Now that we had turned to the surrogacy option, we had a half-dozen prospects.

The next few days were busy. I was called in on a case at the hospital which required four consecutive daily visits to test a highly anxious and depressed young woman. Somehow, I'd always been able to put aside my personal concerns when I had to attend to the needs of my patients. Now, a part of me wanted to scream, "I've got my own problems." A larger part of me, however, was grateful for the distraction. Psychological evaluations demanded tremendous concentration—something I had trouble with that week. There were so many data to integrate, like an abstract jigsaw puzzle. I don't know how I did it.

That week, we put in a new telephone line with its own distinctive ring dedicated to callers responding to our ads. We called it the "baby line." After a few days, the baby line finally rang. It was our seventh caller since we started advertising. It was from a woman with a two year old. She seemed to feel uncomfortable speaking with a man. She repeatedly asked for my wife. She even offered to call back in the evening when she thought my wife might be there. This was an awkward moment, as I had not wanted to tell strangers in the first call that we were a male couple. I felt trapped. I didn't want to lie and yet I didn't want to disclose. Having received so many responses in the last week, I was feeling kind of cocky. I told her I wasn't married but living together with the same person for thirteen years and that we were both doctors, hoping that would make the impression I was trying to create. Finally, I told her that we were men. You might have thought I said we were aliens from another planet! She said before hanging up, "Well, in that case, I'm not interested. Goodbye."

I felt sorry that she felt that way, but despite my regret, I didn't personalize her rejection. She didn't know us as individuals nor did she know our potential as parents. I guessed she was prejudiced— acculturated to the same stereotypes and myths about gays as so many other people. If nothing else, the episode made me think twice about coming out over the telephone again. If pressed, I might simply decline to discuss things further until we could meet. I supposed the majority of prospects would be disqualified, either by us or by themselves.

My attention was directed to lesbian Catherine. I was anxious about our meeting the next day. We had arranged to meet with Catherine and her best friend in my office. I had a good gut feeling about Catherine's potential and I was looking forward to our interview. I remembered the moment we both came out to each other; there was so much relief.

Catherine and Peri arrived precisely at the appointed hour. Smiling, a bit nervous, Catherine was heavy-set—a little beyond Rubenesque—with a creamy clear complexion, strawberry blond hair and blue-green eyes. She was dressed in bright primary colors, wearing a loose top and slacks with necklace and earrings. Her friend, Peri, was a short but voluptuous beauty dressed in black from head to toe. Peri was also a lesbian, divorced, and with young children. Peri and Catherine seemed to have a close friendship, one that felt more like mentorship than lovers. Catherine was obviously buoyed by Peri's active participation in our conference. Peri seemed to care a great deal about Catherine and stressed her own role as the devil's advocate in the process, wanting to be sure her friend knew the risk of bonding with a child during pregnancy.

Catherine was the oldest of four children born to a mother who was sixteen when she married and began having children. She told us that her mother had had four children by the time she was twenty-one. She knew little of her father as her parents had been divorced when she was quite young. She described her family as a "welfare family," noting that her mother often struggled to get food on the table for the children. Notwithstanding their difficulties, she seemed to have a very positive feeling about the family, recalling how they had all pulled together to survive. She recalled staying up late to assist in the laundering work her mother took on to support the family. She felt very close to her mother and siblings due to this early interdependence. Regarding her sexual/romantic orientation, she indicated that her earliest feelings were for other females. Entering puberty, she first came out to her sister, who was repulsed, and then to her mother, who did not reject her, but felt she would grow out of it. At present, however, everyone in the family was supportive of Catherine in her lesbian identity.

Catherine currently lived with a younger sister. She had worked for the past three years as an aide in a residential center for handicapped women. One of her charges, a sixty-five year old blind woman who had been very attached to her, had just died. She had taken care of the woman for three years. She related this story by way of trying to illustrate her experience of loss and how she had been able to cope with it. I privately wondered if this recent loss had any association with her current wish to have a baby.

She told us that she had always thought she would like to have children of her own. Realistically, she wasn't sure if that would ever happen. Currently, she felt it would not be right or fair to have her own child, because she didn't have the money; her situation was not suitable ("I'm living with my sister"); and she was not in a stable relationship. It seemed clear that her experience in childhood had convinced her that children should grow up in a household with two parents and adequate financial resources.

Catherine had been pregnant once before at age seventeen. She did not explain the circumstances but we both knew from personal and professional experience that young homosexuals frequently experiment with the opposite sex in an effort to conform to the majority or to confirm their same-sexed orientations. Her mother was adamantly pro-abortion and compelled Catherine's younger sister to abort a pregnancy at age fifteen. Knowing this, when Catherine became pregnant she fled to Virginia on the advice of relatives to a home for pregnant teens. There she planned to have the baby and give it up for adoption. She related how she fantasized about the people who would adopt her child. She was under a doctor's care during this period, but miscarried spontaneously. The miscarriage was physically difficult, but she didn't indicate that she mourned significantly for the loss. Catherine told us that this was not her first consideration of surrogacy. Three or four years earlier she had explored, then abandoned the possibility with a woman from California.

Catherine discussed her interest in having our baby with her family. Her sister and brother were supportive. Her mother was ambivalent, telling Catherine she would feel bad about never knowing her grandchild. Despite her mother's ambivalence, Catherine believed that gay people should help each other. She seemed to feel that by giving her baby to a gay couple, she would be helping the whole gay community.

Catherine proved to be intelligent and thoughtful. She had obviously thought a lot about surrogacy since we spoke by telephone. Her desire did not seem impulsive nor did she seem immature. Her main motivation, it appeared, was altruistic. She seemed disinterested in the financial aspect. We did not get the feeling that she was trying to make a good impression, although she did ask how many other potential surrogates we were considering, as if she were concerned about losing out to the competition.

Sam and I were so excited about Catherine that we completely overlooked the fact that she had never carried a child to term. She could not give a truly informed consent. Before we realized this, we had compiled a list of her strengths and weaknesses, just as we had done with Louise. Among others, we found Catherine to be responsible, mentally healthy and to have a good social support system.

It was hard to be objective when we were so excited about having a baby. We weren't even pregnant yet I could feel it about to happen. The night before we called some of our closest friends to share our excitement about Catherine. That night I dreamt that Catherine had our baby on my mother's birthday.

As I thought more about how we would establish our parental rights to the baby Catherine might bear for us, it became clear that we would need legal assistance. Although not illegal, surrogacy contracts were against public policy in Maryland and would not be enforceable in court. I wouldn't want to do all that was required to have a baby only to have a judge refuse to grant us custody. One gay legal guide suggested that we do most of the work ourselves and hire an attorney to review it. Recalling Oscar Wilde's ruin, his advice reverberated within me: "Beware the Law."

Chapter Seven

*A*pril finally arrived and the forsythias were a wild profusion of yellow. The daffodils trumpeted in the magnolia and rhododendrons. I derived much joy from watching nature reawaken and seeing the fruits of our ten years of labor in the yard. It now seemed that all that work—the clearing, the planting, the pruning, the fertilizing—was ultimately preparation to create a home in which we could raise our family. Now, our search for a baby seemed so similar...planting, nurturing, basking in the glow of its beauty. It felt like a time of new beginnings within as well as outside our home.

On Sunday we invited Tim and Scott and their daughter, Kati, for brunch. Tim and Scott were a couple from Washington who called us in response to our ad in their local gay paper with kind words of encouragement about using a surrogate mother to have a child. Kati, the product of such a surrogacy for this couple, was now one year old and they were every bit the proud parents. They hauled out their two albums of baby pictures, from pre-birth baby shower to Kati's first step. They inspired us and served as an example of the kind of family we could be. It was nice to know we were not the only ones in the world facing this particular challenge. I wondered how many other gay male couples were attempting to build families.

In our afternoon together, we discussed the perils of adoption, including their use of an unstable surrogate mother who changed her mind frequently. It sounded like hell, but they had remained ever-hopeful and it had worked out in the end. They considered the possibility of a role in Kati's life for her birthmother, something we had ruled out but were now rethinking. Perhaps our surrogate mother would need or want an arrangement like that. If that were the only way that we could have a baby, could we accommodate such an arrangement? We didn't think so.

After our brunch with Tim, Scott, and Kati, candidate Number Five called back. Kathy had received "The Letter" and our references. To my surprise, she was undaunted by our being gay and believed that if we were a loving, stable couple we could be good parents. In our previous conversation, she had told us that she was 5'7", 140 lbs, with brown hair and blue/green eyes. She had graduated from high school and was a homemaker. Kathy believed that being a surrogate would enable her to give the most precious of all gifts; she said she was starting to cry as she described that. She told us her husband was interested in the money. She said she enjoyed being pregnant; she liked "the feeling that something's in there, alive, something God gave me to hold for a while." We arranged to meet two days later.

Hope buoying me with optimism, Sam and I arrived a few minutes late at her apartment complex. It was a run-down cluster of three-story brick buildings, marginally maintained, in a working class suburb of Baltimore. Kathy opened the door with her son, a cute blond toddler who was quiet and inquisitive at first. She invited us into her living room, which was dominated by a large entertainment center. The TV was tuned in to a game show. An infant lay on the living room floor in a new, oversized one-piece pajama. We later learned that virtually all the furniture had been donated and that the family was living on welfare.

Kathy had regular features and all-American good looks. Dressed-up, she could be considered beautiful. Likewise, her children were Gerber kids. We were heartened that from a physical point of view, she made good babies. She seemed nervous at first, as were we. What does one say to a total stranger who might bear your child? She said they were friendly with their neighbors who were also a gay couple. During our two hours together, Kathy seemed to be on her best behavior. She gave the impression that she saw this as a job interview and was motivated to be chosen.

Unfortunately, Kathy's family lived hand-to-mouth. The rent was overdue every month and was not paid until they received eviction notices. Her husband, a landscaper, had trouble keeping a job. The car was not working. She expressed her conviction that her husband was supportive of her being a surrogate mother, even though she described him as macho. We were concerned about their poverty, not wanting to exploit a desperate family. We left with mixed feelings but agreed to meet again later that week. We took Kathy's application and, with her informed consent, administered some psychological tests, just as we had done with Louis and Catherine.

My preliminary screening was comprised of standardized personality tests: the MMPI (Minnesota Multiphasic Personality Inventory), the NEO Personality Inventory, and, in Kathy and her husband's case, the Marital Satisfaction Inventory. I also gave each candidate the verbal scales of the Wechsler Adult Intelligence Scale. I wanted to make sure that our candidates had at least average IQ's. If we were going to go the adoption route, we wouldn't and couldn't be "picky," but choosing a surrogate mother was, in some ways, like choosing a wife or husband. We felt compelled to look at the genetic "raw material" of the candidate. Having a child of at least average intelligence would make him more like his fathers.

Between the application and those tests, I would have enough information about each applicant to assist me in determining their psychological suitability. Unfortunately, as with predicting successful parenting, there is no psychological test battery which could predict a successful outcome in surrogate motherhood.

The next day we would have another meeting with Catherine. Saturday, we were to meet with Kathy and her husband. By Sunday, we should have all the information we'd need to make a decision— preliminary test results, applications, and two interviews each for Louise, Catherine and Kathy. Since both Tara and Laura had disqualified themselves, our pool consisted of these three candidates. I found the screening process difficult. I was tempted to assemble a panel of psychologists to assess each application. Reviewing the scientific literature had yielded little that was helpful in determining how to screen surrogate mother candidates. I called surrogate attorney's offices in Michigan and Los Angeles, requesting to speak with a psychologist familiar with screening surrogates.

There was so much risk associated with using a stranger, so many things that could go wrong. I felt that the weight of the whole process rested on my shoulders. The Michigan lawyer refused to refer me to the psychologist with whom he consulted but said he would call the psychologist and have him call me back if he wanted. That psychologist never called. However, I succeeded in reaching a counselor at a surrogate parenting agency in California. She was very helpful in speaking about their screening process. She claimed they had never had a surrogate renege and gave me a great deal of advice on what to look for.

"First," she said, "never consider a surrogate who hasn't given birth. Such a woman cannot give informed consent." With that one statement, two thirds of our serious candidates were disqualified. She further said, "The typical surrogate mother candidate's primary motivation is to make a unique contribution. The motivation for money is almost always a minor concern." She added, "It's best to solicit and value the husband's participation in the entire process as much as he is comfortable. It's also important for the husband and wife to have a good, open relationship."

Further, she explained the need for young children to understand the surrogacy process. Kathy and her husband would have to explain to their three year old that Mommy was having a baby for us. He would have to know where the baby would be going to quiet his imagination. He should hear an explanation in a way he could understand why Mommy would be coming home from the hospital without his half-brother or half-sister, but that the baby would be safe and sound. He should be reassured that Mommy and Daddy loved him very much and had no intention to give him away, too.

Concerning psychological testing, the California agency used only the MMPI to screen out gross psychopathology. Most of the surrogates screened themselves in or out. The counselor encouraged us to look for the surrogate's support system and, especially, to look at who might be against us in this undertaking and thereby affect the birth mother's decision to go through with the relinquishment. The counselor indicated that the birthmother could pull out at any time unless and until she became pregnant. At that point, there could be no turning back.

Two days later we received a letter from Kathy. She seemed excited about becoming a surrogate mother and was ready to start at any time. She even said she had started taking her basal body temperature. My attention had now shifted from Louise and Catherine to Kathy. She was the only married candidate who had already had children, the only one who could give informed consent.

When I analyzed her psychological tests, her profile revealed both strengths and weaknesses. In the balance, though, it suggested that Kathy could be a surrogate mother. One of the personality inventories showed a non-neurotic person: very low in hostility, low in depression, low in self-consciousness, and very low in impulsivity and vulnerability. According to that test, Kathy had an extraverted personality, high in warmth and very high in excitement-seeking features. It also showed a very open personality with a vivid imagination and an active fantasy life. Her results suggested she enjoyed new and different activities and had a high need for variety in her life. It was likely that she was interested in intellectual challenges and in unusual ideas and perspectives. People with profiles such as Kathy's are generally liberal in their social, political and moral beliefs. Her responses to problems were more likely to be adaptive, flexible and self-sacrificing than to present a defensive facade of superiority. Her profile was also typical of people prone to discount physical problems and minimize the severity of somatic symptoms and medical complaints. In health care situations, it might be important to check for problems even if she reported no difficulties. Unfortunately, it is easy to fake a good result on this test, which Kathy may have done.

The results of her MMPI, a well established test of psychopathology, were more ominous. She had two significant elevations on scales labeled "Psychopathic Deviancy" and "Mania." Part of the difficulty in evaluating my own surrogate mother candidates was that I tended to minimize their psychological deficits because I so greatly wanted each of them to work out. The elevations in Kathy's profile suggested the absence of a deep emotional response (good, in that this woman wouldn't experience grief deeply), inability to profit from experience, and disregard for social mores (also good, in that this business of being a surrogate mother for two gay men defied more than one of the social mores.) Her profile suggested a characterological deficit—she had a personality disorder. It revealed that she was likely to be moody and resentful, although this was generally not apparent at first. People with similar profiles tend to get in trouble with their families rather than the law. Some are antisocially aggressive—they steal, use alcohol or drugs excessively, and may be sexually irresponsible. Such profiles also suggest impulsiveness, resentful attitudes towards authority figures, poor work and marital adjustment, delinquency, and acting out as the main defense mechanism. I wrote another letter to Simon.

Dear Simon,

I just had to write you. I miss you and I haven't even met you! We're getting closer every day, please don't worry...we're coming. You're going to be born next year. You're going to be a healthy and strong baby. And we're going to be the best parents we can be, I promise. Kathy's anxious to make you, as are we. When you come, you'll be in a cradle by our bed. I will hold you as much as you need, and rock you, and make you feel secure and confident. I will learn to change your diapers without cringing, believe me. And I will learn from you...about innocence, about love, about patience, about growth. And every day I love you, I will remember my mother and my father and what it was like to be loved by them...and pass that on to you. I pray that your Great-Grandma will be alive long enough to see you come into this world. 'Til the next time.

Your loving father, Dad

Our second meeting with Kathy and our first with her husband was that Saturday. It was a rainy afternoon when we rang the bell fifteen minutes late, smiling anxiously as we waited for the door to open. Kathy answered the door and seemed warmer this time. She introduced us to Stuart, a big man of 6', approximately 220 pounds in football-type shorts and tee shirt. He had a baby-faced youthfulness about him, yet, because of his size, he appeared older than his twenty-three years. Kathy busied herself making tea while we took our seats in the living room. There was an awkward silence. Three-year-old Stuart junior was as curious about us as he had been the first time and warmed up to us more quickly. He remembered Sam's beeper and was able to make the light go on, proudly showing us his accomplishment.

Both Kathy and Stuart seemed to have difficulty getting to the task at hand, so I steered the conversation toward the prospective surrogacy. We had brought them some pictures of our life, including our home and relatives. I chose pictures of us interacting with all the children in our lives—our nephews and nieces and godchildren. I also brought Sam's "Thank You" book, an album filled with thank you cards and letters from Sam's patients and their families. This seemed to impress Kathy and Stuart, as did our few pictures of the house and land.

Stuart was not a verbal guy; he was more like a jock. He admitted that he had been confused and leery at first when Kathy told him about answering our ad. He had not understood that it would be one of Kathy's eggs that would be used. Now he did. He seemed to warm up to us fairly quickly. Ironically, it was he who seemed eager to make a good impression. I guess having two doctors in his living room impressed him more than the fact that we were a gay couple wanting to inseminate his wife so she could have our baby. He said he thought that you could find no better parents than two doctors. He remarked he thought that we were both handsome, concluding we could make a beautiful baby with Kathy. When we asked how he would feel having his wife carry another man's baby, he said, "I'm getting used to the idea." We also asked how he would feel about refraining from sex until a pregnancy resulted from artificial insemination. "That won't be hard," he said. "We're practically doing that now anyway." This was the first hint of marital discord and my psychologist's antenna started vibrating.

They talked about their relationship, agreeing that finances were their biggest problem, something this surrogacy could help out. However, the Marital Satisfaction Inventory they took suggested that they had more problems than just finances. The results showed elevations on most scales of marital satisfaction, suggesting that this was a marriage with significant problems in virtually every area: finances, sex, emotional communication, problem-solving communication, time together, agreement over child-rearing, etc. Certain allusions to separation were not lost upon us in that first meeting. However, when we discussed how the surrogacy might affect their relationship, they both said they thought it might bring them closer together.

The longer we talked, the more obvious it became that this couple was overeager to make a good impression by saying what they believed we wanted to hear. We acknowledged that Stuart would play a pivotal role in supporting Kathy through the process and that we had to view this as a four-person team. At the end of our three-hour session, Stuart said that he understood a whole lot more about what this would involve and that he was more comfortable with the idea than when we started. "I think you'd make good parents," he pronounced.

During our time together, we observed the younger of their two children crawling around on the floor playing with a number of balloons, toys belonging to the older child. Each time the baby girl would crawl up to a balloon, she would attempt to put it in her mouth. At that point, Mom or Dad would take it away out of fear that it would pop. During the time we were there, I picked up the younger child and fed her a bottle. Kathy seemed grateful for the help. Stuart, Jr. engaged me in a game of catch with a balloon and demonstrated a remarkably good throwing arm. He also seemed to enjoy sitting in Sam's lap and looking at pictures. Both Sam and I had the impression that these parents were overwhelmed with child-rearing and stretched to the limits of their capacity. I sensed that they were on their good behavior and that they would probably correct the children more rudely when company wasn't around.

Before we left, Kathy returned the Surrogate Mother Questionnaire we had designed [see Appendix 1]. Her essay answers were perfect and seemed to reflect the thinking of the typical surrogates I had read about. She articulated that she would not be carrying "my" baby, but "your" baby. She said she wanted us to share in the responsibility of caring for it prenatally and to be present at the birth. She would want minimal contact after the birth, perhaps limited to viewing photographs at Christmas, and to be notified of changes of address in case of medical emergencies.

We were more convinced than ever that this was not a person who would renege on her promise. I did not get the impression that she would have a deep emotional attachment to a child she would have for us. She seemed more dependent on Stuart than in love with him, and both parents agreed they did not want or need more children in their lives. If they did, we believed they would want their own, not someone else's. The major drawbacks were Kathy's characterological flaws and the couple's poor marital relationship. Dare we enter into such an important partnership with an unstable couple? My head said "no" but my heart said "anything to get a baby."

Curiously, they expressed an interest in playing cards with us. They liked pinochle and would like to learn to play bridge. We acknowledged that we wouldn't be friends under ordinary circumstances and stressed that the purpose of our relationship was for them to make a baby for us and for us to pay them for their services. However, we agreed that we should be friendly. Maybe playing cards was one of their tests for us.

Despite the contraindications, we decided to proceed. We had to draft a contract, get a lawyer for Kathy, find out about health insurance, call a birthing center and an obstetrician, and get Kathy to start charting her cycle. We also had to get blood tests for Kathy to be assured she was not already pregnant and that she had no communicable diseases, including HIV. We brought her a basal body temperature thermometer and I gave her the information from one of the many books in my "baby" collection on how to determine when ovulation takes place. I gave her a basal body temperature chart and was privately amused that I could teach her how to use it. I also told her about a national study on surrogate parenting from a book entitled, *Surrogate Parenting*, by Amy Overvold (Pharos, 1988). I thought it would help her to understand that she was not alone in this and that her reasoning was sound; that it could be a good thing for her as well as for us. We left planning to talk again the next Wednesday.

Chapter Eight

*I*n mid-April we took a break from the stresses of surrogate
mother hunting to go to Phoenix and Palm Springs for a
conference and a vacation—both were wonderful. While in
Palm Springs, I had two birthing dreams in one night. I was
psychologically preparing for fatherhood. In the first dream, my
favorite aunt was giving birth to our child right before my eyes. I had
a feeling of exaltation and overwhelming love and excitement at
witnessing this miracle. In the second dream, I again saw the baby's
head crowning, about to be born. This time, the woman was a
surrogate mother. I wasn't sure if it was Kathy. However, the same
exhilaration filled me on awakening.

While we were on vacation and checking for messages daily,
I discovered that Kathy was afraid she might be pregnant. I groaned
when I heard the message played back on my answering machine.
Another setback. Would they never stop? When we returned and
talked to Kathy, she told us she got her period that night. She had
started to chart her period starting last month, so it appeared that she
was cooperating. They had been using condoms, but she said she
was not going to engage in any further vaginal intercourse until she
conceived by us. It seemed to have been as much of a scare for her
as it was for us.

Soon after we returned, we met with Marla, our attorney.
Marla was a thirty-five year old professor of family law whom I had
met when we both were on the Board of Directors of a local AIDS

organization. Our attempts at creating a family were of more than academic interest to her. A lesbian, Marla had been adopted. She and her lover were also exploring alternative ways of creating a family.

Marla had done quite a bit of homework. We were learning together. What she lacked in clinical as opposed to academic experience, she made up for in conscience, trustworthiness, and gay-affirmativeness. We were convinced at that moment that she did not know what she was doing, but that she knew how to find out. At this point, we had to create a contract which would have a chance of standing up in court.

We decided to delay our first insemination until Kathy's next fertile period, which should be around June twentieth. I hated waiting. I could see the disappointment in Kathy's face when we told her, but it was wiser to plan out our strategy completely beforehand rather than after the fact.

The metaphor that came to mind when I thought of the events that were unfolding before us was a theatrical one. We were producing a play in which there was a director, actors, and critics. The lawyers would be the directors; Sam, Kathy, Stuart, and Ken the actors; the courtroom was the stage; and the judge and adoption social workers were the critics. This had to be a very carefully staged production and it was imperative that the script be completely finished before we began rehearsal. Marla told us that there might be a problem with the court's allowing a single parent to adopt the child of a married couple. She also indicated that there was a better chance if we went for custody than if we went for adoption. That was where I felt Marla had yet to learn something—she didn't yet know how this script should end. I supposed in a worst-case scenario we could just take the baby and raise it and trust that Kathy would never come back. Or we could get temporary custody, which was easy, and wait a long time to finalize the adoption—such a long time that the court would be hard-pressed to disallow it. But Marla frightened us with talk of the conservative nature of our local family court judge, who by now had developed into a fearsome image in my mind: the man who was going to prevent me from keeping our baby. I prayed that we would complete all our preparations by the second week in June. The feeling of internal pressure to have this baby was becoming increasingly compelling.

I told Kathy we would be prepared to go over a contract line by line with her and Stuart at our next meeting. Kathy said she thought the contract should say that if the child turned out to be twins, we would definitely take them both. She also said her husband wanted the obstetrician to perform the insemination procedure, not Sam. Aside from those two concerns, they remained enthusiastic about going forward.

While we waited for the contract to be drafted, I began to experience doubts and fears about making this baby—a reproductive version of buyer's remorse. Funny, though, when I named him Simon, there was no doubt at all. It was as though he was already alive and part of our lives. I didn't even consider he might be a she. When I thought more about that, I knew in my soul that the baby's gender didn't matter to me—all I wanted was a child.

When I mowed the lawn one day in the midst of this process—a three hour job—I thought about how having a baby would change our lives. I didn't think I could mow the lawn any more, it would hurt the baby's ears if he rode with me and I couldn't leave him alone. There would be so many things I could not do. While he was young, I'd have to have him within sight at all times. It would be as though we'd be attached (at least while he was awake) by an invisible cord, tethered to each other while I was in charge. I found myself resisting the thought that this would be an intolerable restraint of my freedom. I reasoned if all the other parents in the world could raise their children, so could I. Look at single parents—at least ours would have the benefit of two parents. At least I could get relief from my responsibilities when Sam took over. We had already agreed that adjusting our schedules would mean that I would take care of Simon in the mornings and early afternoons and Sam would take care of him until it was time for bed. This would allow both of us to maintain our practices.

When I honestly considered my doubts, I wondered whether I'd be able to have the empathy and selflessness to put the baby's needs above my own; whether I'd be able to do considerate, nurturing, maternal things like sewing buttons back on clothes or do enough stimulating, educational things with him to enrich him as he grew. Would I rely on television as a babysitter? One of our friends allowed her children only one hour of television per week. Could we do so with Simon? How would we help him fill his time constructively? Neither of us had training in early childhood education.

I thought of the things I would be sacrificing: going out to nice restaurants, spontaneous outings with friends. With a baby, everything would have to be planned. A babysitter would have to be engaged in advance. Certainly, my political activities would have to be curtailed. Sleeping in on the weekends? Kiss that goodbye, I guessed.

I also realized that these inconveniences were a small price to pay for the joy of being able to nurture a life for the short time until he would be independent. And the wonder of it all—his growth and development—discovering each stage of his childhood together. I knew this baby would teach me as much about life as I would ever teach him. This child-rearing was going to be a very reciprocal process. I wrote to Simon again.

Dear Simon,

We're getting closer! This past week I gave a draft of our contract to Marla, who said she would be our lawyer to create you. Although she is going on vacation, she said she will study it and talk with Tim and Scott's lawyer. Tim and Scott had little Kati by a surrogate and plan to have another child. With luck, we'll all be going through our pregnancy together. No doubt you'll be getting to meet your "cousins" as you grow older. Uncle Tim wants to have a "stroller brigade" at Washington's gay pride day parade this year...would you enjoy that when you're old enough?

Are you being a good soul? Are you being patient? I can still hardly wait for you to come. Your birthmommy candidate is cooperating nicely and realizes how much

*you mean to us. As I count on my fingers now, with
any luck, you'll be here next March!*

Please, God, please; let Simon come to us that day.

Love, Dad
(not to be confused with your Daddy Sam)

In the middle of May, Kathy called. Their telephone had been disconnected. She was calling from a roadside phone booth with her two children. She said she just wanted to say, "hi," but I think she needed reassurance that we still wanted her to have our baby. The wait seemed interminable to Kathy. She said Stuart was complaining that not having intercourse was getting on his nerves. I reassured Kathy that we were still interested, thought of her every day, and were waiting as eagerly as she for the day of insemination. I asked if her fertile period had arrived the day before, as we had calculated, but she felt it hadn't come yet. I encouraged her to continue monitoring her cycle. She said she was really "preoccupied" with this surrogacy job whereas Stuart was beginning to feel left out. I made a mental note to make sure to include him in our next meeting. I told her that she should call me in a week to check on the progress of our contract.

At our next meeting, I planned to go over the contract with them, which would include all the details of the adoption process. We would address their questions and concerns, negotiate, and then amend the document as necessary. At that time, we would arrange a meeting between them and their lawyer and our lawyer, and then begin artificial insemination. I was full of fear and excitement.

Two days later I talked with Marla at length. She had begun to feel that we should not use Kathy and Stuart. Rather, she thought we should go either for an independent adoption or find an unmarried woman to be our birthmother. She said that even if we went to court with all parties consenting, we might not get the judge's approval for this arrangement. We were scared to go through the courts, knowing that they were not disposed toward surrogate mother contracts or gay people. Yet if we didn't, the child could be snatched away from us at any time. No matter how many ideas came up during our brainstorming session, no alternative was without its risks.

Then, as if I weren't struggling with enough doubt, talking with some friends made matters even worse. Our friend, Kai, an adoptive parent of two, expressed her concern about our intent to enter into a surrogacy arrangement. I struggled to listen with an open mind and not be defensive, but I felt anger at her negativity. Kai talked about the baby's need for his or her mother and how our baby might feel deprived, different, eventually even resentful about the terms of our surrogacy arrangement. She mentioned the word selfish and said she thought our desire to have children outweighed our consideration for the welfare of the unborn child. She was concerned about our use of a surrogate mother rather than adopting. She felt that while adoption would be looked upon by society as an unselfish act, one in which both parents voluntarily gave up the child, and we stepped in to save a life, in surrogacy, we would be bringing a child into the world planning on depriving him of his mother. She didn't seem convinced that having two fathers could compensate for having no mother. She barely allowed that having two parenting figures was better than having one—or that we were the same as any infertile couple who wanted a baby of their own.

I was torn. Kai said things which were difficult, even painful for me to hear. Defensively, I thought, "Why should we consider our friends in our decision-making?" Yet we loved and trusted our friends, most of whom were well-educated and many of whom had children of their own. Kai suggested that I speak to other close friends and invite them to share their views candidly, something I did. Fortunately, the other couples with whom I spoke were unconditionally supportive.

I wrote a letter to Kathy and Stuart in which I told them that we were agonizing over the conflict between our deeply felt need for a family; our deepest belief that we could offer a child a wonderful life; and our hidden fear that society might hurt our child because both his parents were men. I told them that we had selected them and that we prayed that they would be able to withstand the demands of the journey and relinquish the baby to us at the end. I wrote that we hoped that, vicariously, they would be able to appreciate our happiness, gratitude, and the indescribable enrichment they will have provided to our lives. We wanted them to know that despite our mutual intentions, the baby Kathy would bear would be legally hers. Although the lawyers were still figuring out exactly how it would be done, she would be giving the infant to two people who would love and protect it and enrich its life in as many ways as possible.

By the third week of May, Marla had completed her legal research on adoption and surrogate parenting contracts as they pertained to gay people. We had a long meeting which was both edifying and discouraging, producing as much anxiety as it relieved. Marla made it clear that using Kathy to have a baby for us would not be the same as a heterosexual couple using a surrogate mother. That was because we would not be substituting my wife with Kathy because the law didn't recognize our marriage. Surrogacies, she explained, involve placing a child with its biological father. It requires a blood test to rule out the surrogate's husband to assure paternity. Surrogacies involve instituting child placement statutes and filing for step-parent adoptions by the biological father's wife. This, then, terminates the birthmother's rights. Finally in control of the situation, Marla outlined our options.

The first would involve taking no legal steps to terminate Kathy's rights. This option would assume that Kathy would step out of the picture as promised, allowing the child's biological father (Sam or me) to raise him. Of course, this would bring with it tremendous risks, for example, Kathy changing her mind at any time after the birth, even years later, and returning to claim her child. Should that happen, we would face a dubious outcome in a custody battle and incur a numbing financial burden. Also, international travel would be difficult as many countries require notarized permission slips from the absent parent for minor children traveling with only one parent.

The second option would be to have Kathy's husband's name on the birth certificate and have them place the child with one of us in an ordinary, single-parent independent adoption. This would be legitimate because a child born to a married woman is presumed to be the product of the marriage, even if the child were the result of artificial insemination. By avoiding placing Sam's or my name on the birth certificate, even though our semen was used, the court would not have to ask the troublesome question, "Why does the biological father live with the adoptive father? What's going on here?" The only unanswered question in this option was how the financial arrangements would be made.

The third option Marla suggested was the one she also recommended. Abandon Kathy and further attempts at having a baby with a surrogate mother and focus on an independent adoption. The down side here was the difficulty we would have finding a pregnant woman who would give her baby up to two gay men. On the up side, once one of us did get custody, it would be permanent after the recision period passed and the petition was granted by the court. With all three options, we could go back to court after a period of time to petition for a co-parent adoption by the non-adoptive partner.

So, we had three difficult options, each with its own risks and potential rewards. The thought of going through the pregnancy and then having legal problems was even more terrifying than the debacle with Amy. On the other hand, with an independent adoption, the birth mother could change her mind at any time and decide to keep her baby. By our not having a biological relationship with the baby, the birth mother would be less likely to feel an obligation to fulfill her commitment. How were we to make such a choice? The road to gay paternity was paved with fear and doubt.

Memorial Day was a weekend of moment. We decided not to take the risk with Kathy. What really convinced me was dinner with David, a psychologist friend from Hopkins who reviewed the psychological tests with me. David reminded me of the unpredictability of people with personality disorders such as Kathy's. I finally realized that I had been so intent in my desire to have a baby and so appreciative of Kathy's willingness to have one for us that I had not been objective in my assessment of her personality. I could no longer deny her longstanding personality problems. She had defects in maturity and judgement and she was impulsive and rebellious. Her character was typical of people who change their minds spontaneously, fail to keep their promises, and rationalize their changed behavior to their own advantage.

So, ironically, we decided to abandon Kathy out of fear that she might abandon us. We feared she might try to keep the baby, not because she might want it, but because she might gain by doing so. It finally sank in that the character of our surrogate candidate was of paramount importance. There were simply too many risks for us to pursue Kathy further. Since we had neither signed a contract nor attempted artificial insemination and since we had told her that any of us could call the arrangement off at any time unless a pregnancy could be confirmed, I felt free to end our relationship.

I dreaded writing to Kathy. I hated to disappoint her and Stuart. The timing was particularly unfortunate because they were on the verge of being kicked out of their apartment for non-payment of rent. I could not tell Kathy that Sam and I doubted her reliability. I would simply say that there was just no way we could legally adopt her baby if we paid them money.

I wrote Kathy a letter in which I told her about our conversations with our attorney and her consultations with family lawyers in the area. They were unanimous in discouraging us from going ahead with a surrogacy. I told her that we also had discussed this with friends, family, and professional acquaintances, and had searched our souls to find the right thing to do. We wanted a baby and family of our own so desperately, we found it difficult to be objective. I said that we tried our best to figure out how to accomplish this surrogacy, but every scenario we hypothesized violated the baby-buying statutes—laws which made it illegal to pay for anything more than legal or medical expenses in an adoption.

Further, I wrote that if we went ahead with what we planned, we could never adopt the baby she would bear for us. The courts would forbid her to give up her rights and responsibilities to the baby and it would grow up in a legal limbo. Not having complete parental rights and the possibility of a custody dispute was too much of a risk for us to take. I told her that we hated to lose her and were concerned for her welfare. I closed by telling her we were abandoning surrogacy, not Kathy, and I thanked her profusely for her participation thus far. I acknowledged that the only way we were going to get our own baby was through a single-parent adoption in which we found some woman, somewhere, who could not keep her baby.

I felt horrible. I experienced saying goodbye to Kathy as yet another immense personal loss. Although I hated not taking the risk out of a fear of something going wrong, the possibility of losing the baby and then having to support it for eighteen years was too compelling to proceed with Kathy. Instead of sending the letter, however, I held it, waiting to see what the next chapter brought.

Chapter Nine

*A*fter Kathy, our thoughts turned back to Louise, the lesbian. Louise was clearly more responsible and psychologically healthy. She had convinced us that, despite her not having had any children, she would not renege on an agreement. We called her again and discovered that she was still interested. She reiterated that her main reason for wanting to do this was altruistic.

She had raised the issue with her therapist, who was also a lesbian. Interestingly, her therapist's lover had just given birth to a baby whom they produced by artificial insemination. Louise said her therapist might not be objective at the moment. It was hard to know if that might work for or against us.

Louise noted that her lover was not supportive of this idea. She believed, however, that her lover would support her in her decision if she decided to go ahead with the insemination. Her lover felt Louise might be seeing this just as a way to have some income while she worked on her education and her career. Moreover, Louise thought she should be paid more money than the ten thousand dollars we offered, but believed we could work that out.

In addition, Louise had been bothered at our second meeting (with the four of us present) by the fact that we did not want her to have any contact with the child. She interpreted this as our strong desire to have the child bond to us as parents exclusively and without confusion. While she appreciated this need and supported it, she felt that children born into such an unorthodox situation would eventually want to meet their biological parent. Thus, she wanted to be assured that we would make that opportunity available to the child if and when the time came. She reiterated that she might enjoy some kind of role as a family relation, e.g. an aunt, but didn't indicate that this was paramount. She said she would like to receive some kind of periodic progress reports, perhaps a video, for instance. She expressed confidence that the lawyers could find some workable way around the legal obstacles, including finding some way to get money transferred to her legally. She had actually generated some creative ideas over the last several weeks as she had continued to think about being a surrogate mother. These included marrying one of us; going out of state or out of the country to have the baby; and being hired by us for some nominal position in order to hide the money. She wanted to have a proper written agreement even though she knew it would not be enforceable. It was important to her that our mutual intent and the specifics of our plans be recorded. Interestingly, she wanted to make sure such an agreement would specify that Sam and I would have custody of the child if she were to die in childbirth. She had visions of her sisters trying to take the child in that situation and wanted to be sure that wouldn't happen. We ended the conversation with our mutual interest in surrogacy reaffirmed and the acknowledgment of the need to discuss the details further with our attorney.

Louise called back that night with two practical questions: How soon did we contemplate progressing with insemination (As soon as possible); and should she get a basal body temperature thermometer? She said she had charted her ovulation before and had no trouble telling when she ovulated. I told her to get the thermometer and start charting. She knew this would help us maximize the chances of conceiving a boy, an idea she supported. Sam and I had long before decided that we would love any baby that came to us, but that if we had a choice, we would want our first child to be a boy, simply because we understood males better.

Among the more fascinating things I had learned in preparing for pregnancy was that men have both boy-making sperm and girl-making sperm. The former are smaller, but faster. If they fertilized the egg, the child would be a boy. If the larger, slower girl-making sperm fertilized the egg, then the child would be a girl. According to one doctor who wrote a book about choosing the sex of one's babies, parents can influence the sex of a child by the timing of the insemination in relation to when ovulation occurs (Shettles and Rorvick, 1989). That doctor postulated that these facts might also help explain why more than fifty per cent of artificial inseminations result in boys. The boy-making sperm, being faster swimmers, get to the egg first.

By the first week in June, we had decided to go ahead with Louise. Her character was more important than the fact that she had never had a baby. But before we had a chance to send the goodbye letter to Kathy, we got an unfortunate surprise. Louise backed out. In a very caring letter, she expressed her regret over not being able to do it. Among other things, she told us that she was simply too frightened:

> ...the minute I first felt a kick from the baby inside I would be hooked. Oh, I'd give up the child as I promised, and work through the grief (probably for the rest of my life) with my friends and work on it in therapy—but the question is, why? Why cut myself open? It's going to hurt like hell, so why wound myself? I would never be able to stop wondering how the child was doing. It isn't that I don't believe in your abilities as parents. You two would be good for any baby. It's just that I can't be the one who helps you make that happen. I know this will disappoint you and I'm sorry, but better now than later when we're really into it.

I called Louise the day before receiving her letter—the day after she sent it. I was strangely detached when she told me over the phone that she had changed her mind. I guess I felt relieved, because she confirmed my greatest fear of using her. Emotionally, she just couldn't go through with a surrogacy. When she told me she had sent a letter about having changed her mind, I felt grateful that she had the foresight and honesty to do it at this stage, before she had become pregnant.

Louise's changing her mind brought me back to Kathy, whom I had so reluctantly given up. I was starting to feel desperate again.

Thank God I hadn't yet sent her the goodbye and thank-you letter. Although I realized the risk was greater with Kathy, her motivation was impressive. She had been aggressively pursuing this job. No one else was offering to have a baby for us. However, I still worried that Kathy was calculating how to attach herself to us forever. Despite this, I continued to think about her. Call it intuition, but ever since meeting Kathy for the first time, I had seen her as the mother of our child. Was I kidding myself?

Marla continued to express concern about Kathy. Without knowing her, she seemed to think she would be trouble. I wanted to trust Marla's intuition, but she had never met Kathy. And I was increasingly desperate with each passing day. Of course, there was still that pesky MMPI profile. Who was it who said, "Denial is not just a river in Egypt?"

We decided on two final screening measures before going ahead with Kathy. I wrote Kathy, outlining the following proposal. First, Kathy would meet with an attorney who would render an opinion as to her suitability to be a surrogate mother. Secondly, I would arrange for another psychologist to evaluate Kathy more formally. I agreed with Marla that if Kathy did not pass the screening of either the lawyer or the second psychologist, we would then disqualify her as a candidate. With Kathy's ovulation just two weeks away, we had a lot to do.

A few days later, I called Kathy at her new waitressing job to ask if she had received our proposal and to inform her of her scheduled appointment with the psychologist on the coming Thursday. She had and planned to call the attorney closest to her home today. She said she might need help in getting to see the psychologist because of their lack of transportation. I offered to take her and Stuart to the appointment, but she told me they were going to borrow a friend's car for the first appointment.

Kathy called me the next morning sounding chipper. She said, "Stuart's getting antsy because he isn't getting laid." Despite this, she was still resolved to go forward. I proposed getting together for dinner with Kathy and Stuart so that we could talk. Kathy thought that would be a good idea because Stuart was still feeling left out. I was so happy I hadn't sent her that goodbye letter.

That afternoon, I had a meeting with the County Executive's

representative about the Baltimore County gay rights bill. I'd done my homework and our meeting was going to be interesting. It hadn't yet become overly burdensome to juggle the gay rights and babymaking efforts simultaneously. Unfortunately, the man was not encouraging, saying that the highest elected official in our county was not inclined to support the passage of an amendment to the civil rights law protecting gay people from discrimination based on their sexual orientation. Despite this, I was determined to personally lobby each of the seven elected officials on the County Council.

The following weekend, Sam and I went to Rehoboth Beach, Delaware, our area's gay summer beach resort. The weather was lousy; it rained each day. On the positive side, we were away from home and all stresses and we got to spend time with our old friends, Greg and Gail and their children, who were also on vacation. It was nice to be away from babymaking concerns for a few days. I had gone to college with Greg and we had stayed in touch over the years, even though he had migrated to the West Coast long ago. I am godfather to their first-born child and appreciated the chance to see my godson and his little sister. Greg and Gail wrote a beautiful letter of reference for us to the adoption agency we had planned to use before Amy changed her mind.

When we came back, I received a call from Kathy. She had to reschedule her appointment with the lawyer because she couldn't get a babysitter. I sensed that she was depressed because of their imminent eviction and Stuart's continued unemployment. Kathy would be moving to a friend's home without her husband. I didn't know where Stuart was moving and I feared this might be more than a temporary separation. Kathy lamented Stuart's irresponsibility and felt trapped. She wanted to find work in order to be more independent, but feared being unable to afford child care. I was cautiously sympathetic, seeing my role more as a caring, concerned bystander than as a rescuer in the drama of their lives. I feared that this impending move might cast the final lot against Kathy as our birthmother.

Kathy called Saturday morning. She had had her appointment with Mary, her attorney, the night before, and had the impression that the attorney felt Kathy would be adequate. I was waiting to hear from Marla to verify that assessment. In case Mary felt Kathy was unfit for any reason, I'd taken out two advertisements in the *Pennysaver* again—one for an adoption and one for a surrogate, in all geographical areas except Kathy's. I didn't want to lose more time if things didn't work out with Kathy.

The next day, I attended a man's funeral, the father of a friend. Even in the face of death or, maybe, because of it, I thought of new life and our journey to Simon. Afterwards, I was moved to write my unborn son another letter.

Dear Simon,

Today, I helped a friend bury his father. He was eighty-seven years old, an immigrant and beloved patriarch of a large, successful Jewish family. It caused me to remember my father's funeral and to think sadly of how much I miss both my parents. It seems that, in the end, all that is important is children, as that is all of value we can truly leave behind. And now my thoughts turn to you, my son. I still wait anxiously for your arrival. I am not sure if Kathy is going to be your birthmother. Sam is distrustful of her and not confident in her ability to do this for us.

I see me carrying you after your birth, helping to wipe away the vernix, rocking you, feeding you, feeling your tininess and anticipating your growth and development with the most profound joy. I continue to promise myself and Sam and you that I will try to be a good father. Saying the old, familiar Hebrew prayers in the synagogue felt comforting. It made me want to go back to synagogue and raise you as a Jew so we can go together and pray and be a Jewish family. Your Daddy and I still need to work that dilemma out.

*I don't know how to make you comfortable as a Jew
unless we demonstrate what that means on a weekly
basis in a fun, loving, joyful way. I hope that if I do,
we can learn to integrate religion into our lives together.
I know it will be a challenge—your Daddy Sam is
Presbyterian. Simon, be patient. We're coming.*

Love, Dad Ken

Marla called the next week. Even though Mary had okayed
Kathy, Marla reiterated her reservations. She was especially concerned about Stuart's unpredictable nature. Mary and Marla agreed
that Kathy should have pre-insemination counseling.

Since Kathy and her children had left her husband, I, too, had
become more concerned about her stability. The previous weekend,
Sam and I decided to wait and watch to see how she got her life in
order. I knew I should call Kathy, but I was reluctant. I feared she
would become angry and that we might lose her as a candidate
without having anyone to replace her.

The next morning I had the sad conversation I'd been dreading
having with Kathy. I expressed our concern about her home,
income, job, and marital situations. There was so much stress on her
now that I feared being pregnant could overwhelm her. In addition,
Kathy said that her attorney frightened her when she said that should
divorce proceedings follow this separation, she might risk losing
her children if she were to become a surrogate mother. I wondered
if her lawyer was being overzealous in her assistance to Kathy.
Regardless, we both agreed that Kathy needed time out to stabilize
her life before becoming pregnant. She admitted that she had
harbored fantasies of our rescuing her and said her mother expressed concern that she might not want to give up the baby if that
was a way she could hold on to us. Of course, it now appeared wise
to postpone proceeding with Kathy, especially since we had renewed our advertising efforts and had received other inquiries.
Without ever sending her the goodbye letter, that phone call became
the unceremonious end of our relationship. I never spoke to Kathy
again.

Chapter Ten

*B*y mid-July, six months after our loss of Amy's baby, we had little to show for all our efforts. A new raft of surrogate candidates surfaced in response to our latest ad and I sent them all "The Letter." It was hard to wait for the responses. The letters sent, all we could do was wait. I suppressed my desire to follow-up with telephone calls.

I'd been feeling depressed at this seemingly interminable delay in moving forward. Marla discouraged us from surrogacy. Sam said he wanted to pursue adoption rather than surrogacy, but was really doing nothing to further our adoptive aims. And all the while the clock was ticking: we were getting older and the age difference between us and our future child(ren) was increasing. My biological clock was not just ticking, it was booming in my ears.

My uncle Lenny and elderly grandmother Fay visited during this low period. I had looked forward to seeing them; they were my closest family after my brother. The visit was short but sweet. Grandma was quite happy to visit me at my retreat as she calls our place. We swam, ate crabs, and reminisced. We were all looking forward to her ninetieth birthday party at our house next month, although I could tell she was a bit nervous. Grandma hated to be the center of attention. While they were here, our new ad in the *Pennysaver* came out. Uncle Lenny chuckled with delight as the phone repeatedly interrupted us as we were enjoying our soak in the hot tub. A market researcher, he was impressed that we could get such an enthusiastic response from a classified ad.

Of the numerous responses we received since Louise disqualified herself and we parted company with Kathy, several candidates emerged. Malvina seemed the most promising. She was older (twenty-five), a definite plus, single, Catholic, a redhead, and had one previous birth, a child she relinquished for adoption three years earlier. She was a full-time nanny who took care of two children and was planning on returning to college in the fall to complete her education. She said her father was a doctor. She described herself as fiercely independent. She told us that her previous adoption had been a good experience. She felt she did something wonderful for the adoptive parents; was very satisfied with her attorney; had not seen the child since; and had no desire to do so. Because she had done it before, she felt she could do it again. We last spoke on Thursday. We agreed I would send her our letter of introduction and application materials and she would call me on Monday after she received them to set up an appointment.

Just in case she didn't work out, I took out the ad again. I expected another flurry of responses and was now preparing "The Letter" assembly-line style. Our word processor was smokin'. Despite the renewed promise of each new round of responders, I was beginning to tire of this fishing expedition and wished our birthmother would emerge. I was also beginning to feel degraded by confiding our personal story to every stranger who expressed a passing interest in becoming a surrogate mother for us. By repeating the same story over and over again, it started to feel contrived and I was beginning to bore myself. I had to keep reminding myself that each person who called was hearing this for the first time and I had to try to be upbeat and optimistic. Again, I took comfort in writing to Simon:

Dear Simon,

I write to you for comfort—I'm still missing you, waiting anxiously for your arrival. I've been wondering about sports...what sport, if any, will be your forte.

There was an article about cricket in the paper this morning and I realize that I will have to encourage you, support you, and teach you things that I, myself, may not know much about. We will learn together, you and I, about how to be a child. I do not anticipate that I will attempt to "remake" my childhood through you -it was all right as it was. I want to give you a rich life in preparation for your life as an adult.

What about summer camp? I went away for eight weeks every year of my childhood. Camp Tamarac. Sam did not although he went to church camp for one week each summer. Will it be safe? Will we risk your being teased if we send you away? Kids can be cruel and we don't want to expose you until you are old enough and strong enough to defend yourself. Maybe we'll find a summer camp for kids of gay parents. Don't worry, son, we'll cross that bridge when we come to it. Hurry home now.

Love, Dad Ken

July turned into August and our fourth ad for a surrogate had just appeared in the *Pennysaver*. We received several calls of interest. Unfortunately, most were from high school dropouts, which suggested either below-average intelligence or character problems. Sam and I arbitrarily decided that high school graduation would be a minimum requirement for considering a caller eligible to become a candidate.

Of the last group, one woman distinguished herself from the crowd. Jennifer was a thirty year old former paralegal secretary who said she was experienced with surrogacy cases. She was white, married to an Asian man and had three kids. She said she belonged to Mensa, graduated from high school at sixteen and college at nineteen. I didn't know whether to believe her or not and planned to check her references carefully.

Tired of wasting time, I came out to her quite naturally over the phone and was pleased with her reaction, which was unfazed. Her tolerance was understandable in light of her interracial marriage. Apparently, she had suffered from some discrimination which had sensitized her to the need for mutual acceptance and respect in society.

I sent Jennifer the application, "The Letter," and our references. Hopefully, we would be able to meet soon. If she passed the psychological tests and personal interview, the next step would be to have her meet with a lawyer.

The following week Jennifer called me back to arrange a meeting. She was challenged and amused by the application and motivated to complete it. Coincidentally, she lived near Malvina, the redhead, with whom we would be meeting the next night.

Unlike Jennifer, Malvina was reluctant to divulge all of the highly personal information we requested without meeting us first. A number of little things had transpired with Malvina which suggested that she might be ambivalent (e.g., she "accidentally" threw out our application and references"). Another fact about this young woman, which concerned us, was that she had given up and lost a baby. Regardless of what she said about the adoption, I knew that giving up a baby was a traumatic life event. Going through another pregnancy could easily reopen old wounds. I wondered if these scars had not yet healed and if they contributed to her ambivalence.

To her credit, she indicated up front when I called her that she wanted to meet before she proceeded. Malvina said she could judge people quickly and would know in fifteen minutes whether she wanted to work with us or not. I gave her our references' telephone numbers and invited her to call them if she wanted reassurance about us. She sounded like an outspoken, no-nonsense type—a knife, however, that can cut both ways. It might prove that her ambivalence would be too great to overcome. We would see. We set up our meeting for Saturday afternoon.

Three hours before we were to leave Baltimore to visit her in Annapolis, a fifty mile drive, Malvina postponed our meeting. She said in her message on our answering machine that an emergency had come up—something to do with her son—and that she would call back on Sunday night. I was suspicious. Sunday night passed without a call back, so I called her Monday morning. When I reached her, she suggested meeting some other night the next week. She told me she was singing at a nightclub on Monday night. She asked, "Can you drop in and catch the show?" Her invitation struck me as inappropriate.

I realized that emergencies happen, living with a physician as I do and taking emergency calls of my own. But this eleventh hour cancellation was suspicious. Furthermore, her reference to her son made me suspicious, as it suggested that she was still attached to him, even though she had given him up for adoption at birth. Even more disturbing, she had invited us to watch her perform out of the blue. It made me wonder about her narcissism, reliability, maturity, and sense of responsibility.

Ultimately, we met with Malvina at the home where she worked and lived as a nanny. We were upset that she was surprised to see us when we arrived after a long drive. She claimed to have forgotten about our appointment and she had lost the second set of application materials I had sent. When we left, we told Malvina that we'd call her if we wanted to proceed, but both Sam and I agreed that Malvina was unreliable and that we should not waste our time considering her further.

Meanwhile, the telephone kept ringing. I began to think of our situation as a gambler playing a slot machine. Most of the time, there were no results; some times a few coins. When were we going to hit the jackpot?

Chapter Eleven

*A*fter Malvina's disqualification, another candidate emerged. Zoe's husband, Mark, called after having received our packet. He said they were very touched by our letter and wondered if they could help us. They had no problem with our lifestyle and were impressed by the letters of reference that we had enclosed with our autobiographical letter as well as the picture of our house.

I knew very little about the couple so far. Married for three years; they both were twenty-four; had two young boys; and worked in responsible jobs. Zoe had enjoyed her pregnancies; had uncomplicated labors and deliveries; and would view surrogacy as lending her womb for nine months. Mark never mentioned money. This was an exciting prospect and I felt optimistic about the afternoon meeting.

We visited them in their apartment in a quiet, well-maintained, middle class complex with a pool, lawns, and trees. They lived on the third floor of the three story walk-up. The stairwells were wide and floored in linoleum, giving the building a plain appearance. Each apartment had its own large wooden balcony.

Mark, a six-foot tall, thin, blond, good-looking young man in gym shorts and tee shirt, opened the door. There was no foyer. The door opened onto the living room, where Zoe sat with her baby. Her two year old son stood nearby, looking suspicious. Zoe was short and a bit stocky. Mark was friendly, inviting us to sit down and offering us iced tea, which we accepted.

It was awkward at first but soon conversation became easier and we spent two and a half hours getting acquainted. After talking with them for only a short while, it became apparent that they were ambitious. Mark worked two jobs and Zoe worked as much overtime as possible at her job as a cashier. Mark was applying for a job with the fire department and had already taken one of the psychological tests I had planned to give him.

They clearly loved their babies and valued children. Zoe enjoyed being pregnant and felt good about helping out another couple in this way. In exploring why she wanted to be a surrogate mother, she recalled an asthma attack the little one had two months after he was born which required hospitalization. Zoe was terrified he wouldn't survive. She prayed to God to save her baby. Giving a baby to a childless couple seemed to be Zoe's opportunity to thank God for saving her youngest. When asked what they would do with the money they received from the surrogacy, they said they would use it as a down payment on a house for their family. Here were two couples contemplating helping each other in their own ways. They would give our home a baby; we would give them a home for their babies.

The evening after we met, Zoe called. She told me they had had a scare. While babysitting, Mark's sister had discovered the paperwork we had sent them which included my business card. Mark's sister told their mother what she had discovered. Mark's mother called him in a rage, swearing that she would not permit this and that she would go to the press in her effort to prevent it if they proceeded. Zoe did not think that his mother or sister remembered or knew our names but could not be sure. Zoe wanted to reassure me that she still wanted to go through with this and Mark said he would support her, whatever her decision. Despite this, the confidentiality of our relationship with this wonderful couple was compromised. We would not be able to continue a relationship with them. We could not risk engaging Mark's openly antagonistic mother. The thought of a homophobic mother-in-law nosing her way into our private agreement and turning it into a media circus was too threatening to allow us to consider Mark and Zoe further. What a sad and unpredictable turn of events. It forced us to turn our attention to the candidate we would be having dinner with the following night in Annapolis, Jennifer.

Chapter Twelve

B y August's end, despite the dozens of letters I had mailed to inquiring callers, we still had no birthmother. Only Jennifer remained eligible. Not long after her call, Sam, Jennifer and her husband, Tad and I met at a Mexican restaurant near their home.

Jennifer was a short, thick woman with an olive complexion, short auburn hair, and pretty, regular features. She was brash, outspoken, funny, and unrestrained in challenging us about things that piqued her curiosity, such as our questionnaire. She had a good sense of humor and didn't take herself too seriously. Jennie had a pad of prepared questions, mainly about why we wanted answers to the various questions in our questionnaire. I found it curious that she seemed more concerned about why we wanted to know things about her than about what being a surrogate mother would require of her. Her guardedness made me suspicious that she had something significant to hide. Tad, on the other hand, was just the opposite: quiet, soft-spoken, and withdrawn, but attentive and bright. His participation had to be solicited and he did not volunteer thoughts or feelings freely.

Jennie had an interesting life. Born in the South, she was the product of an affair between her mother and a native American. That accounted for her olive complexion and somewhat rounded features. Jennie had not learned this until her adolescence. Her parents had divorced early in her life and she had been reared by her father and step-mother. She did not explain why her father had custody of her. Always a good student, Jennie became pregnant in her last year of high school. She described the father as "a doorknob." After high school, she went to a university while caring for her daughter.

After college, Jennie married a policeman and got her first job as a medical assistant. Soon after, they relocated to Georgia, where Jennie continued her employment in the medical field. The marriage didn't last. After her divorce, she moved again, and worked for another doctor until she met and married her second husband, Tad. When I checked her references, the doctor gave her a glowing report, saying he would have her back in a minute.

Jennifer said she had learned about adoptions and surrogacy through part-time work at a law firm. She felt adoption was a wonderful thing. She was close to people who had been adopted and she knew that, because she was born out of wedlock, she, herself, might have been adopted. She saw surrogacy as the opportunity to help others out and make some money at the same time. Although she didn't see the amount we were offering as a great deal of money, she didn't ask for more.

Probably the most troublesome and potentially insurmountable obstacle for us in this case came out accidentally. She told us that her mother had a chemical imbalance that required her to take medication. The story she told made it sound as if her mother had had a psychotic break. During this episode, her mother called at all hours of the night, talked nonsense, and was confused and disoriented. I wanted to see a copy of her mother's medical record, if possible.

Jennie expressed ambivalent feelings about being a surrogate mother. She wanted to help out, but was hesitant. Was she afraid of pregnancy, of being unable to relinquish the child, of passing on a genetically compromised baby? Might Tad want to keep the baby? Were we not offering enough money? What? She said she had mailed in the psychological testing materials, so I would be able to learn more about this woman's psychological makeup later.

Two weeks later we had a second visit with Jennie and Tad at their apartment. We met their kids, all three beautiful and healthy-looking. Jennifer was late for our 7:30 p.m. appointment and arrived brimming with the difficulties of her day at the retail store where she was an assistant manager. She seemed unable to put a lid on it. We could virtually see her mind working as she seemed to say everything that wandered into it, without filtration or inhibition. Unfortunately, her talkativeness raised the questions: would she be able to keep our relationship confidential? Could this loquaciousness be symptomatic of a mental disorder?

Her husband, constitutionally quiet, was not quite so reserved as he had been in the restaurant the first time we met him. He was casually dressed in tee shirt and shorts and there was a quiet, good-natured quality to his personality. Clearly, he was buoyed but overshadowed by his wife's extraverted nature.

We talked about how we envisioned the pregnancy and birth would proceed. When Jennifer learned that our attorney had suggested that we not put Sam's name on the birth certificate, she got angry at the law and society and said, "Well, I'll go to another state!" She was fiercely independent and seemed readier to argue something than to acquiesce, a trait I saw in myself as well. We had brought and then read aloud our first draft of the contract. She saw things going much the way we did and seemed satisfied with most of the details.

Still, there were several sticking points, one of which was that she had changed her mind and now said she did not want us to see the delivery of the baby. She was shy. Tad exclaimed, "But they're doctors!" but that did not affect her objection. She seemed reluctant to expose herself to us, physically as well as emotionally. Could we have such an important relationship with such an intensely guarded person?

A few days after our second meeting, we had a telephone conversation with Jennifer. She explained how strongly she felt about maintaining her privacy. She didn't send back her application right away because she did not want to reveal that she had been arrested for grand larceny several years earlier. That a false accusation led to her arrest was confirmed by her former employer, whom I called. Gratefully, she said, "Jennifer was an excellent employee. I'd love to have her back. Jennie virtually ran the office, did everything except sweep the floors, handled all the bank accounts including my personal bank account." In all, she gave her an excellent reference.

We planned to go ahead with Jennie. She said she would ovulate in eight days, but we agreed there was not enough time to do everything we needed by then: have her evaluated medically and psychologically and prepare all the legal work, etc. She said that she would be happy to see our obstetrician and we decided to include a mileage allowance in the contract, as well as the cost of her medical insurance through work. I felt happy, excited, and scared. Jennifer was going to be our birthmother.

Chapter Thirteen

September was a busy month. Grandma's ninetieth birthday party at our house was a smashing success. My brother, five first cousins, two uncles and I, planned a catered, sit-down dinner for fifty of Grandma's closest relatives and friends. My step-sister belly-danced in full Arabic costume but the climax of the affair was when the variety of children, grandchildren, great-grandchildren, and other friends and family members recited their testimonials to her in the living room while the rest of the party listened, laughed, and cried. We had compiled all of the speeches into a "Memory Book," which we carefully bound and gave to Grandma at the party. In those short speeches, we thanked Grandma for all the happy memories that she had given us, some seventy years old. A sad moment came for me when it was my turn to read my contribution. I acknowledged my mother's death and how much we all missed her, particularly my grandmother and I. However, most of my memories were funny or affectionate. I liked the house being full of people that day. Thirteen relatives stayed at our home with the rest staying at a nearby hotel for the weekend. The party-goers took up an entire floor.

The affair was especially welcome in that it distracted us from the nail-biting anxiety of waiting for Jennifer to get her medical and psychological screening exams while watching her fertile period go by. I was determined that our first attempt at artificial insemination would be in October, as we had missed September's ovulation. I hoped her slowness was truly due to her busy schedule and not her ambivalence. She called that week to share that Tad wanted us to know that they were $25,000 in debt from credit card purchases and the money we were planning to pay was a significant motivator for them to proceed. Of course, this raised the question about whether Jennie engaged in a pattern of pathological overspending, something which could be symptomatic of the hypomanic mental disorder I had suspected. Did Jennie have the same illness as her mother? We anxiously awaited the results of the psychologist's evaluation. In our last conversation, Jennie had reiterated her eagerness to get started. She didn't relish being pregnant in mid-summer, which was when the baby would be born if we waited much longer.

In the middle of all this, the gay rights drive in Baltimore County I was so actively involved in was heating up. We constantly had to address attacks from the homophobes of the local religious right. Happily, after much debate and public hearings, the Human Relations Commission recommended amending the law in our favor. All that was left was lobbying sessions with the seven County Council members who would be voting on the issue. I wondered what people would say if they knew I was trying to have a child. It was hard to keep this a secret.

By the third week of September, Jennie and Tad were still keeping us in the dark about whether they wanted to proceed. We had no signed contract when we finally got the psychologist's report. Dr. Deame found significant sociopathic tendencies in our surrogate mother. Just what we didn't want to hear. I knew it was better to have everything out in the open beforehand, but I was disappointed with her findings. The report ended with a wise word of caution, "I hope you don't let your yearning for a baby cloud your judgment." I hoped not, too. Or was it too late? I resisted calling Jennifer and Tad, not wanting to put pressure on them. The ball was in their court and I just had to wait for them to call. I hoped my attorney would hear from their attorney soon. I hated this adversarial feeling, with each of us having our own attorneys. Sam felt we could wait a month if we couldn't get all the paperwork done by the time she ovulated. Marla said the attorneys were poised for a signing, but I was so nervous and pessimistic, I doubted even her.

I hated feeling so out of control. God, why couldn't we have a baby by ourselves?

Jennie called us the last week of September to say she had just started her period. Prior to that, she thought she might be pregnant as she was over a week late. That meant we had fourteen to seventeen days until ovulation—Sam's birthday. We cancelled our cabin-in-the-woods-weekend, confirmed our sperm concentration laboratory appointment and planned to abstain from sex from October fifth until Insemination Day.

As Murphy's Law dictated, the lab we planned to use to perform the sperm concentration had only one technician trained to do that particular procedure. He would be on vacation exactly the days we anticipated Jennifer ovulating. Damn! Nothing was easy. We could not go to the other fertility lab close by without lying about our marital status, because they only took infertile, married, heterosexual couples. The only other lab in the area was in Virginia which was too far.

Our plan was to mix our sperm in a cup, have the lab concentrate it in a machine and place it into the glass straws normally used for artificial insemination. We wanted to concentrate the sperm to sort out malformed cells and to decrease the overall volume so that it would approximate an amount typically found in a male ejaculate. We arrived at this solution for romantic as well as practical reasons. We wanted to have our own child, which logically called for the co-mingling of our semen. On a more practical level, we agreed that mixing the ejaculate would be the only natural way of deciding who would be the biological father.

Other bad news—the lawyer Marla had pre-screened for Jennifer had not responded despite Jennie's repeated attempts at calling. I could only guess this was the lawyer's way of letting everyone know she was not interested in this case. So, we went to the next attorney on our list. That was Nellie, a feminist and former government attorney whom we met at our adoption class several months back. Nellie and her husband had just succeeded in adopting a baby. I was happy for both of them. Their success gave us hope. In my hopefulness, my thoughts turned to Simon:

Dear Son,

I feel you getting closer. You're like a lost bird circling high in the sky, coming closer to earth, to the North American continent, to Maryland, to our home in Baltimore.

I think about you daily, how we're making you— we're doing the best we can—but you already know that. I feel your excitement at preparing to be born. It's less than a year away. I feel it. We're going to have a good life together in our family. You'll be special, unlike the other kids you'll know, but that will remind you that you are loved, not that you are different. You'll be loved and cherished because you are special and never a day will go by that when you go to sleep you won't be grateful and happy that you were born into our loving hearts and home.

Love, Dad

We met with Nellie, her husband, and their new baby at their home in Baltimore. Nellie was very interested in helping us succeed in having a child with Jennifer. Their baby was gorgeous. As we talked, we discovered we had interesting connections. Aside from having mutual friends, knowing their doctor, and having taken the same adoption course, they had visited our home when a mutual friend housesat for us a couple of summers before. Nellie said she would be happy to represent our surrogate mother if that woman felt comfortable with her.

In our conversation on Thursday night, Jennifer said she had not mailed the contract back to me, but that she could go over the changes by phone if I wanted. I agreed because it would save time and we spent an hour on the phone going over her suggestions. The majority were grammatical and pertained to form rather than substance. I acquiesced to every concern. At the end of our conversation, we had an agreement. I told her I'd send her the amended document and she could go over it one last time with her lawyer before signing it.

Jennie expressed some concern about having to travel the fifty miles to Baltimore to see an attorney. I said that if we tried to find another attorney closer to her home, we would most likely miss this ovulation. However, I told her it was her choice. In my opinion, the advantage of using someone who was already familiar with the case seemed to outweigh the disadvantage of having to travel the one hundred mile round trip once or twice, especially considering we would have paid for her expenses. We ended the conversation with my saying I would call her back after I found out from Nellie whether she would take Jennifer on as a client.

The next day I called Jennie and gave her Nellie's home number. When I got home that night, I found a message on the machine from Jennifer saying that she called the number twice and got a very rude person on the phone who said she had the wrong number. Would I please call her back with the right number. Confused, I called Jennifer back the next morning and got Tad, who said Jennie was lying down. He took the two numbers I gave him for Nellie and relayed them to his wife.

Two hours later, I got a call from Nellie saying she had not yet heard from Jennifer. I was perplexed and disappointed as I had already given Tad the numbers and Jennie had said yesterday she would try to see Nellie today. I suggested she might want to try Jennifer. She did, and called me back to say Tad told her Jennifer was lying down and would call her back. This, too, was strange, considering how anxious Jennifer appeared to be to talk to an attorney. Annoyed by this contradictory behavior, I was too close to the situation to realize that these were signs of the sociopathic traits the psychologist described in her report. Was this foreshadowing problems we would have with Jennifer down the road? Nellie called me back later, saying she had finally received a call back from Jennifer, that they talked for an hour, and that Jennie agreed to come later that afternoon.

What Nellie then shared troubled me. She said she had a great conversation with Jennifer, and that Jennie had indicated that she liked us both and thought we would be great parents. Jennie, however, said that she was feeling pressured by me, that she had some changes she wanted to make to the contract, and that we were forcing her to use our lawyer rather than her having her choice! I was flabbergasted, even though Nellie reassured me that overall Jennifer was quite positive. Nellie informed Jennifer that she was wrong about having to use Nellie as her lawyer. If, after their meeting, Jennifer did not want Nellie to represent her, she would bow out.

I was disheartened to hear these comments. Until that moment I would have characterized our relationship as quite good. I would have said we had excellent communication. Hearing her tell another person she felt pressured by me just didn't ring true. Either she'd been lying to me or lying to Nellie. I took this as an ominous sign.

This report from Nellie confirmed that I had to back off. I would let the lawyers hash things out and not try to be an intermediary. I hoped Nellie and her clients' meeting would go smoothly. Nellie's impression was that they hit it off on the phone and she really seemed to want to help make this happen. We would see. There were eleven days left until we anticipated Jennifer's ovulation and we were counting every day. I was blind to the clouds that a more objective person might have seen gathering on the horizon.

Jennifer called me Sunday night. I was on a friend's boat and retrieved the message from the answering machine remotely. I had agreed to do a radio interview that night about the gay rights initiative. I called Jennie back after the interview. I hoped she hadn't been listening—I didn't want her to think that I was a "public figure." Irritatingly, Tad said Jennie couldn't come to the phone. More approach-avoidance?

Sam called her back later. It turned out to be a question about using the predictor kit we had given her to time her ovulation. Jennifer believed she might ovulate as soon as this Friday. We were anticipating it to be next week. I prayed her HIV test would be done; our contract would be finished; and the artificial insemination consent form Marla was working on for Dr. Shelly would be completed in time.

Jennie called Monday night. She said she was joking with her daughter about how they would tell us we were pregnant, perhaps by sending us the positive indicator stick in the mail. I suggested skywriting from a plane over our property. It was a good conversation which suggested that she had resolved whatever ambivalence she was feeling and was ready to proceed.

I felt good knowing that the details had been ironed out by the attorneys. One caveat was that Tad didn't want his name on the birth certificate. Jennifer wanted it to read, unknown. That seemed all right with Marla, rather than having Sam's name on it. Technically, we wouldn't know who was the birthfather. Also a concern which had yet to be ironed out was Jennie's smoking. She had not stopped while pregnant with any of her children and it was unlikely she would stop during this pregnancy. We made an offer to pay for Jennifer to take a smoking cessation class. I felt terrible about her smoking while pregnant, but realized that any pressure on our part to control her smoking would be likely to backfire. I called the American Lung Association and had literature sent to her about their programs.

Marla and Nellie worked well together, having been colleagues in the past. Both were committed to making this work. They knew we were determined to proceed with Jennifer's artificial insemination this cycle and that her ovulation couldn't wait. I prayed that it would occur early so that the lab technician we needed wouldn't be on vacation. I-Day was less than a week away.

The next morning I received an excited call from Jennie telling me she started testing herself for ovulation and the liquid turned pink. It was not quite the shade the literature said indicates ovulation within twelve to twenty hours, but it also allowed that some women's samples don't turn as dark as the example in the instruction booklet. She could ovulate within the next two days. She was concerned we wouldn't be able to do it because her HIV test wasn't completed. Not having the HIV test done, we agreed, should not stop us, as her risk of infection was so low. She agreed, however, that the contract would be nullified if the result was positive. I was concerned that the contracts might not be finished and we'd have to wait yet another four weeks. God, this was exciting and annoying. Marla said to me that they were poised to go as soon as Jennie got to the lawyer. Well, that was five days ago. We might miss this ovulation. That would mean Jennifer's possibly being pregnant next August. Please, I prayed, don't let Jennifer ovulate before

Sunday or Monday. I felt myself becoming more anxious by the hour.

A week later was day fifteen of Jennie's cycle. We hadn't heard from her since she had called excitedly the week before saying her test was pink. She had dropped out of sight. I scurried around like a madman getting the contract to Nellie from Marla and getting Sam to sign it and then mailing it to Jennifer, all with the expectation that she would be ovulating any day and we might miss it if she didn't sign it in time. She said she had gone in for her HIV test last Wednesday, but we hadn't received the results or proof of her insurance yet. Worst of all, Monday, Tuesday, Wednesday came and went without a word from Jennie. What the hell was going on?

It was maddening that she had built us up for this ovulation. By the following week, we still hadn't received a call. It now seemed that she had abandoned us. We called Nellie, who said Jennie had appreciated our not calling her and asked us to have patience, that she was still with us, operating in good faith, but that she just had not ovulated. After talking with Shelly, who had gone to quite a bit of trouble to get the supplies necessary for an artificial insemination, I learned that Jennifer may be anovulatory—not producing eggs. Apparently, when she was off the pill, Jennie's cycle was quite irregular and she might not ovulate for two or three months at a time. We felt disappointed and deceived. Maybe we shouldn't have gone this far with someone with her personality traits. Maybe we shouldn't have been in such a rush.

Because of what Nellie told us about Jennie's remaining interest in doing this, we were willing to wait, but it was important that we get verification from Shelly about her medical condition. He indicated that he might have to prescribe medication for her that would induce a period and then continue with a fertility drug to induce ovulation. Of course, that brought with it the risk of a multiple birth.

I felt angry and disappointed. I decided if Jennifer showed any more bad faith I would renew our advertising. Sam said it was premature to give up on Jennifer, but I continued to feel distrustful and impatient, my biological clock ticking away like Big Ben. I had also been thinking more about adoption and quitting our attempts at surrogacy.

Columbus day brought Sam's thirty-ninth birthday. We spent a lovely weekend at Deep Creek Lake in western Maryland with Dave and Tom, two of our closest friends. We had a wonderful time despite the lousy weather. We played golf, rode horseback, ate great meals at country inns, played bridge, swam, jacuzzied, and drank celebratory toasts. We also attended the Autumn Glory Festival of Garrett County, which was a small-town parade complete with home-baked goods, clowns, and Shriners on go-carts. Even Miss Maryland was in attendance. We decided to go on this weekend after it became clear that not only was Jennifer not ovulating, but she had not signed the contract. Sam said he felt a bit misled because she had not indicated an anovulatory condition. I had been waking up early each morning since we'd been away, anxious that she changed her mind about going through with it (despite Nellie's assurances that she was operating in good faith), or wanted more money, or some other such thing.

The following week, Jennifer was supposed to meet with Dr. Shelly to explore inducing ovulation chemically. I was anxious to know where we were headed. Nellie said Jennifer wanted us to be patient. It would be easier for me if I knew that we were steadily progressing toward our goal. Would Jennifer consent to such medication? So far, she had not inspired me with confidence in her commitment.

A few days later I called Jennie. She wasn't home. I spoke to Tad, who said Jennifer was having second thoughts, despite the fact that the contract was rewritten to her satisfaction. He cited the demands of her job. Apparently, she was recently promoted and was beginning to wonder whether getting pregnant now might prevent her from fulfilling her work obligations. He recommended I call back when she got home at 5:00 p.m. I called at 5:35 p.m. and spoke to her eldest daughter, who told me her mother wasn't home. She said that she would tell her to call me when she got home. Frankly, I didn't believe that Jennie wasn't home, and I didn't expect her to call back. I feared we had lost her despite all her declarations of solidarity. I was disappointed and angry that Jennifer not only wasted so much of our precious time but lacked the courage and responsibility to admit her change of heart to us directly.

I felt strangely detached. I suppose I felt like crying and like screaming in anger simultaneously. I was disappointed. I thought Jennie's absence reflected her ambivalence about undergoing this pregnancy and my guess was she was too immature to have thought through the implications for the long term. Now that she was facing artificial insemination, she was running scared. It was easy for her to say she wanted to do it as long as it remained something in the future. Now that it was here, she was backing off. I knew she was entitled to change her mind. In fact, if she did not resolve her ambivalence, I would not have wanted her to proceed. I just wanted her to tell us up front. The next day was Thursday, the deadline for the *Pennysaver* classifieds. With a sigh, I called to resubmit my ad. We never saw or spoke to Jennifer again.

Chapter Fourteen

The third week in October, I put the ad in again. I also called Kimberly, a woman who had called three months earlier expressing interest in being a surrogate after she delivered the baby she was pregnant with at the time. She was twenty-seven, married to a Navy pilot and sounded healthy. She told me she had delivered last month and had been thinking a lot about us in the interim. After I came out to her, she told me that she had guessed we were gay. She said she was still interested in reading our letter of introduction and looking over the application. I sent them to her on Friday and hoped to hear from her soon. I never cease to be amazed at the number of women who contemplate being a surrogate mother.

That weekend, we attended the birthday party of a friend and ran into many people who knew we were trying to find a baby and who were curious about our progress. I became depressed repeating our sad stories over and over. I knew I didn't have to share the bad news, but it helped to talk to others as well as to write in my journal. I remembered the lesson from our adoption class—tell as many people as you possibly can that you are looking for a baby, because one of them just might know a woman who is looking for a couple to adopt her unwanted baby.

Out of desperation, we sent a short note to Jennie and Tad expressing our desire to meet with them and our hope they were still considering surrogacy. As each day passed and we hadn't heard from them, I became increasingly resigned to their abandonment.

Every time I thought we were starting all over again, my heart sank. In spite of my unhappiness, I never lost confidence that Simon would come to us, just that it wouldn't be through Jennie. Through whom? When will you come, son?

The following week we went to the theater to see "Park Your Car in Harvard Yard" starring Jason Robards. We were delighted to see our friends Dr. Shelly and his wife in the audience. We had a drink with them afterwards and spent a lovely couple of hours visiting. They were quite curious about our babymaking endeavors and I was saddened to have to tell them our disappointing news about Jennie. I needed to remind myself that our disappointments were our losses, not our shame. It was more difficult for Sam to share our disappointments with others.

The next day, people started calling in response to our latest ad, which had come out the night before. Of the six calls, I mailed "The Letter" and questionnaire to the three new candidates who qualified. It was both exhausting and revitalizing to start over again. But my philosophy demanded that we plug on until we reached our destination, no matter what the obstacles. In the meantime, Sam and I started talking about reconsidering a single parent adoption.

On October twenty-ninth I woke up crying from a dream. I was on a beach by a raft, competing in an archery contest. A baby was tied to a pole on another raft 30 feet away with a sponge in the middle of its forehead. We were to take aim at that baby. I shot my first arrow and it missed, going into the water. No one in the audience or the referee had any hesitation, nor did it appear that there was any danger to the baby. My opponent shot his arrow. He was a fellow cub scout from my childhood who was murdered in early adulthood. It landed right in the middle of the baby's forehead but did not hurt the baby. The arrow was removed and it was my turn again. This time, instead of shooting up, from the beach, I got on the raft so I was at an equal elevation with my target. I put the arrow into the bow and started shaking. As I tried to pull the string taut, it became clear that this was wrong, that the shot could kill the baby and that all the adults around this baby were being irresponsible. I stepped down without shooting and went to the mother, who seemed unperturbed, telling her I couldn't do it, that we were looking for a baby so hard that I couldn't possibly risk killing one.

I broke down on her shoulder, crying over my emptiness.

As if on cue, later that morning Kimberly called back. She was the woman who had called me earlier in the summer interested in having a baby for us after she had delivered her own. I had called her back last week. She told me she and her husband were overawed by our letter, references, and questionnaire. After a long conversation, she said they decided against it because we were homosexuals and she felt God hated homosexual acts (not homosexuals). Her uncle was gay and she had gay and lesbian friends, but she could not go against her conviction, no matter how much she felt a baby could benefit by living with us. Annoyed by her response, I found myself wondering if she felt this way about gay people, why did she request our letter of introduction and the application knowing that we were gay from our previous conversation? Although not a terrible blow, this call, even sensitively handled, reinforced our catastrophic fear about adoption and surrogacy. People called upon their prejudice against gay people to make judgments about how a baby would fare under our care and about Sam's and my suitability as parents. I hated being disqualified without even being known.

I called Nellie, Jennifer's lawyer, later in the morning to ask her to call the social worker from the agency they used for their adoption to explore whether they would work with gay people. She said she would. In addition, she said she'd follow up with Jennifer tomorrow, if only to put closure on our relationship, and would call me back then.

Chapter Fifteen

B y November twenty-second, we had mailed twenty-two letters to callers from the last three classified ads. We were now
advertising both for a surrogate mother and to adopt an
unwanted baby. Two of the most interesting calls came from two
pregnant women—Theresa and Sandy.

Theresa was black; her boyfriend was white. Theresa was four
months pregnant. I talked with her at length and found her to be a
charming, soft-spoken girl with a decidedly British accent (English
nanny) and said I would pass her name along to someone I knew
who wanted a mixed race child if we decided against it. I came out
to Theresa and it didn't seem to make a difference to her. Perhaps
that's still the lesson in all this—to act as if our homosexuality was
not terrible news, but as if it's the most natural thing in the world.
But it was Sandy who became my obsession of the moment.

Wednesday night we received a call from Nancy, whose best
friend Sandy was thirty-eight weeks pregnant and wanted to give up
the baby boy (who was due any day) for adoption. My head swam
as we talked. She said they had been working with another couple
who changed their minds three weeks earlier and had not yet found
suitable replacements. Nancy had seen our ad in the *Pennysaver*. I
did not risk coming out to her on the phone. We made a date to see
each other at our house on Sunday but after talking with Sam, I
called back to arrange an earlier meeting considering how close she
was to delivering. Sandy had antepartum testing today at the local

hospital and was four centimeters dilated. They anticipated she would deliver the baby this Thursday, Thanksgiving Day.

Nancy told me a little about Sandy. Sandy was an Amerasian refugee who escaped to the United States as a child. Although traumatized by the horror of war in her country, she was eventually adopted by an American family and the balance of her childhood was normal. She said her boyfriend was handsome and Caucasian, but now out of the picture. In fact, he didn't even know that she was pregnant. I was forced again to consider adopting a baby who might not look like us racially. It didn't take me long to conclude my desire for a child was stronger than whatever concerns I had about raising a child who might look different from his or her parents. I also felt that a child who was three quarters our race would look sufficiently like us to avoid the problems often encountered among children raised by racially different parents.

We faced a dilemma. I didn't want to do anything to lose this opportunity, for example, come out over the phone. But Nancy asked about my wife, a question I deflected with practiced ease. I wrote a letter shortly after hanging up with her, but just couldn't mail it. I figured we would tell her in person when she came. I woke up at 4:30 the next morning, anxious about this meeting. This early morning awakening continued to occur whenever something exciting, good or bad, was going on in my life.

Sam was his usual patient self. When I asked him how he felt, he said, deadpan, "I'm very excited." He was my rock while all I felt like doing was laughing and crying at the same time. However, I also experienced panic, recalling Amy and the beginning of this journey last January. Her story was so similar. Amy, too, called out of the blue, nine months pregnant. Everybody tried to accomplish all the paperwork necessary for an adoption at the eleventh hour. Then, Amy changed her mind in the delivery room under the influence of that overzealous social worker. The despair when we went home empty-handed was numbing. Then, terrible grief and rage followed. It took me months to recover from that episode.

How could I let myself enjoy this excitement and anticipation when it was so tentative? Sandy and her baby could slip away at any moment like waking up from a dream. Every time I started to feel happy and optimistic, I remembered those hours in the hospital, thinking I would be cuddling Amy's baby later that day only to go home empty-handed and confused. What if Sandy didn't want a male couple? It would certainly be understandable. I would try to convince her that we would be excellent parents, as if I could sell ourselves as best for this child. How could anyone do that and how lasting would such a sales pitch be? Did I even really believe it myself? That, given a choice between a straight couple and a gay couple, I would want my child placed with a gay couple? So what if we're happy and healthy, bright and secure? We're homosexual! Writing Sandy a variation of "The Letter" calmed me:

Dear Sandy,

I was so excited by Nancy's call that I had to sit down and write. What came out was this letter to you. Sorry about the typing, but if you knew my handwriting, I'm sure you'd thank me.

How can we thank you for your expression of interest in considering us as adoptive parents? There don't seem to be words to describe these feelings. First and foremost, more than anything else, know that it is our most profound desire to parent a child. Nancy's call came not only as an answer to an ad, but as an answer to our prayers. We have wanted a child for years. We can only try to understand how emotionally difficult it must have been for you to have made the decision to relinquish this baby for adoption.

By these letters of introduction and reference and through our meeting/s, we hope that we can demonstrate to you that, should you decide to place this baby with us, he will have a happy, privileged life. He will know love, caring, guidance, support and have deeply committed parents and extended families and traditions which were passed on to us and which we would like to pass on. First, more about us.

Sam and I were raised by our biological parents in healthy, happy families. My father was a successful businessman and my mother was a homemaker, social worker and author. Sam's father is a retired school

principal and active in other community affairs. His
mother is a retired elementary school teacher. Our families love us dearly, as we, them, and their greatest wish
for us, too, is to have children. (Sam's Mom's last card
to us said, "I haven't had a grandchild in eighteen
months...hint hint").

We are an attractive, healthy (HIV negative), Caucasian, stable couple. I'm forty-one and Sam's thirty-
nine. I'm from New York and Sam is from San Diego.
We met while graduate students in San Diego thirteen
years ago. After a wonderful fifteen month courtship, we
began living together. Since that time, we have considered ourselves married. We have every legal connection
married couples have—all by contract: wills, powers of
attorney, joint ownership of accounts and our home, etc.
Our relationship is excellent and we are both committed
to spending the rest of our lives together. You would
need never be concerned about the stability of this
child's adopted family.

Both Sam and I are distinguished in our professional careers and take great pride and pleasure in
helping others. As you know, I am a licensed clinical
psychologist and Sam is a board-certified family practitioner with a sub-specialty in gerontology. Those who
know us like and respect us. We are happy people who
lead productive lives and have no regrets except our
childlessness, which we pray we will resolve soon.
Approaching mid-life, we realize more than ever that
helping others is not enough. We have so much to give,
we believe children in our life will make for a very
happy, healthy, and complete family for all of us.

We are active in our communities and have many
friends. We value family and friendship highly. So that
you may understand more fully how we are perceived by
others, I am enclosing copies of four of the many letters
of reference we received last January for the adoption we
were counting on which fell through at the last minute.
Please feel free to call any of these references.

We love children and cherish the precious time we have with our nieces and nephews, god-children and friends' children. As I told Nancy on the phone, our child will have full-time parenting as we will adjust our schedules when the baby comes so one of us is with him at all times. As professionals and as caring individuals, we realize how important it is to provide consistent positive early experiences for children. We are ready and waiting to do so. As someone who has been to college, I think you can understand how we can offer a child a lot of advantages. He or she would have the best education available, which is something both of us value highly. Our child would have swimming and tennis here at our home and the chance to grow up healthy and active with plenty of room to run around and play. We would provide opportunities for developing natural talents in the form of music, art and/or dance lessons, etc. As we have done extensive international travel, we could also provide travel and vacation opportunities which would enrich any child's life. Our home is large and comfortable. It overlooks a wildflower meadow on over five wooded acres bordering a 115 acre farm in suburban Baltimore county. I am enclosing a picture as you might naturally be curious.

What kind of people are we? We love board and card games, sports, theater and opera. We enjoy gourmet food, singing and playing the piano. We appreciate the value of hard work and mental and physical discipline and health. Landscaping and gardening are two of our favorite hobbies. We have tamed half of our property over the years, clearing and planting the meadow, orchard, garden and hundreds of decorative trees, shrubs, flowers and bulbs. We love working and playing outside and go to the beach several times a year. Keeping us company with all this are a cat, a dog and a parakeet.

We appreciate the sensitive nature of adoption and understand that as mature, responsible adults, we must make profoundly important decisions in the best interests of the child which will affect his entire life. We are prepared to make and keep such commitments. We only ask that you be as honest and open with us as we are with you. God knows we do not want to go though another devastating disappointment as we did last January.

Maryland law allows adoptive parents to pay for legal and medical expenses associated with the pregnancy and adoption. Of course, we are prepared to do so. If necessary, we would be able to arrange private medical care with the obstetrician of your choice. Technically, the adoption would be a single-parent adoption because of our marital status. However, we have a co-parenting agreement waiting to be signed once the baby is born which details our joint responsibilities and obligations as co-parents. We are also waiting to change our wills, estate plans, etc. We anticipate that our child will have a hyphenated last name. For your information, I've already applied for our formal adoptive home study with a private agency.

Nancy, you were unaware when you called that we were a male couple. We can only trust that you believe as we do—that people should be judged by their character—whether they are good, kind and loving people or not. We hope that by meeting and becoming acquainted, you will have a positive feeling about us and the life we are prepared to offer this baby. We look forward to seeing you soon.

With warmest regards,

Ken Morgen, Ph.D.
Sam Westrick, M.D.

Sandy and Nancy came over to our house that Sunday before Thanksgiving. They were two very attractive, beautifully dressed young women. Sandy did not look as if she was going to give birth in five days—she was so small. Only her obvious discomfort—her hand often going to her belly and making frequent trips to the bathroom—gave away the proximity of her due date. We talked about Sandy's pregnancy. We talked about the birthfather and asked if he was going to consent to the adoption. Sandy was going to lie on the birth certificate and say unknown—a plan which worried me. I noticed that Nancy did a lot of talking for Sandy. Her story, although not atypical of young women with unwanted pregnancies, was different from the other stories we had heard.

Sandy was born in Vietnam and raised in orphanages until the fall of Saigon, when she was transported by air to the United States and sent to a series of foster homes. She suffered many disappointments in those homes, thinking she was going to be adopted each time, only to be sent on to the next. Finally, she was adopted by a large family with both adopted and biological children. One of her sisters was gay. She worked nearby as a salesgirl but had been on pre-maternity leave for two weeks as the due date approached. She told us she definitely didn't want the baby and wanted to give it up for adoption immediately after birth. She didn't want to see it or to hold it after the birth.

The father of the child was a former boyfriend. The relationship ended badly and she claimed the father did not know she was pregnant. Sandy intended to keep it secret. How could I tell her this wouldn't be acceptable in court? She said she was touched by our inviting her and Nancy to our home, as most other couples they interviewed wanted to meet in neutral places.

At first, Sandy and Nancy were quite surprised that we were a male couple as our ad had referred to us as two doctors. By the end of our interview, however, Sandy gave me a tiny shopping bag with the word "Baby," in little building blocks, artfully drawn on it. It had a stuffed animal inside and a card addressed to "Mommy and Daddy." Receiving it, I felt both touched and despairing. There was a sense of unreality. Even though she said in words and by this action that she wanted to give us her baby, I couldn't believe it was true. Cynically, I wondered how many such bags she had in the car. As if she could read my mind, Nancy said, "Sandy's been carrying around that bag for the past three weeks. She's been waiting to give it to the parents who will adopt her baby." Was this heaven or purgatory?

By the end of the Thanksgiving weekend I felt lower than I had since we were abandoned by Amy. Without a word of explanation, Sandy and the baby disappeared. When I called the hospital to search for them, I was told that Sandy delivered on the twenty-seventh as expected and she and the baby were discharged on the twenty-ninth. We never found out what had become of Sandy or the baby. Sandy never returned any of my many telephone calls. As with Jennifer, I felt hurt and angry. We were abandoned again. I was so wrapped up in my own pain, that I could not appreciate the suffering Sandy must have been going through.

Adding to our despair, our close friend Al took his own life on the Tuesday before Thanksgiving. We were shocked, confused, and deeply saddened by his death. Although we knew he was depressed, he had started taking medication and said he was going to enter psychotherapy. I had even given him a list of names to call.

I struggled to find meaning in his death, but there were too many unanswered questions to achieve peace. I had never lost anyone close to suicide before. With Sandy gone, Al dead, another potential adoption floundering, the gay rights bill in trouble, and no surrogates in sight, I was bereft. Al's death tested my threshold of tolerance for loss. For the first time in my life, I took a tranquilizer to help me calm down and sleep past five or six a.m.

After Sandy fell through we received calls from several other prospective birthmothers. One, a thirty-one year old waitress and single mother, was pregnant thirty-eight weeks with twins and wanted ten thousand dollars to give them up for adoption. Another was from a woman in our neighborhood who wanted to put her biracial newborn up for adoption. A third with five children also fell through when she and her husband decided to keep the sixth child she was carrying.

Then, we received a response from another candidate who returned her application in the mail. Sandra was a twenty-three year old single woman living with her boyfriend and three small children in central Pennsylvania. She really seemed motivated. After talking with her at length, studying her application and letter of introduction, I assessed her intellectual potential to be in the low average range. That was a disappointment. Even though she had graduated from high school, we had already decided we wanted our candidate to have at least average intellectual potential. Yet, I was torn. We couldn't afford to eliminate any possibilities. But in my heart, I felt that despite Sandra's obvious qualifications, we would not seriously consider her.

Chapter Sixteen

The Christmas holidays passed uneventfully and it was now New Year's Eve. Although no one knew it at the time, it was one week before my son would be conceived. It had been no busier a Christmas season than normal, although every chore seemed to have taken greater effort. I just couldn't muster the energy to send out Christmas cards. Unenthusiastically, I managed to buy presents for everyone on my list. My stack of "Case Closed" files of surrogate and adoptive mother candidates was now four inches thick.

Sandra, the single woman with three children in central Pennsylvania, remained very anxious to be a surrogate mother. Our reservations about her low-average IQ and her poverty remained. Despite these drawbacks, she was cooperative and responsible, filling out all of our forms, sending us pictures of herself and her children, all very attractive. Sam and I were sufficiently impressed with her resolve and planned on seeing her when we returned from our winter vacation.

Some of the people we encountered on our journey to find Simon were very kind. Some were not. The week before we left for vacation, two more women expressed interest in becoming a surrogate mother for us. Both of them withdrew. One of them, Dee Dee, a thirty-nine year old married mother of four didn't even have the courtesy to cancel our appointment. She just didn't show up in spite of the fact that we had confirmed it that very morning.

Several days later, I spoke with a single social worker friend from "adoption school" who said that the agency she had been working with assigned her a four month old girl from Russia. She told me Russia had opened up for foreign adoptions in recent months and that we might be able to get a Russian baby with little or no wait. I filled out and mailed in the requisite Immigration and Naturalization Service forms just in case. The incessant ups and downs of hope and disappointment were getting me increasingly depressed. One day we had a baby, the next day, it was gone. One day we had a surrogate, the next, she disappeared and we were back to reconsidering adoption. I didn't know how much more I could stand.

The one year anniversary of our loss of Amy's baby boy came and went. I'd been mopey, even though we spent a week on vacation in Puerto Vallarta. As if the heavens conspired with our luck, it rained most of the week. Then, two days after we returned home, we received three calls from prospective birthmothers. One was from a woman already pregnant; one was from a surrogate candidate; and one was from the step-father of a fourteen year old girl who was seven months pregnant. The pregnant woman, a twenty-one year old divorcee, changed her mind before we ever met, leaving the pregnant minor and the new surrogate candidate.

Larry had called me once before, about a month ago, saying that his daughter needed ten thousand dollars to cover medical and psychological expenses associated with her unplanned pregnancy. It seemed that he was more interested in getting someone to pay for his child's maternity expenses (he had no insurance) than to find a good home for her baby. He wanted to talk about money over the phone, which I thought inappropriate. My gut told me to stay away from this family and steer them toward an adoption agency. But I agreed to meet with them and invited them to our home the next Wednesday afternoon. I was troubled by what sounded to be either mental illness or mental retardation in this girl and I wanted to assess her intelligence. I didn't tell Larry that we were a male couple. This was going to be interesting.

When the doorbell rang it was Larry, his wife and their fourteen year old daughter, Shana, arriving promptly at the appointed hour. I answered the door, deliberately asking Sam to stay in the living room so they wouldn't turn and leave before even entering the house. We were quite nervous about their reaction to seeing that we were two men. Shana, a quiet, nervous girl who looked her tender age, was due in seven weeks. She was fair-haired and had blue eyes. She sat quietly, letting her parents do most of the talking. The parents were well dressed, Larry in a tie and jacket and his wife in a business suit. They seemed eager to make a good impression. Apparently, Larry was being pressured by their doctor to pay his daughter's medical bills. Shana was aware that she was going to have a baby very soon. She seemed to realize that neither she nor her parents could care for her baby and that she had to give it up for adoption. However, she seemed reluctant about doing so and I had the feeling that she had some longing to keep it. She expressed fantasies about staying in touch with it through yearly letters or photographs. The family, although surprised, appeared unfazed that we were a male couple, a fact we briefly acknowledged at the end of our hour-long interview. Our time together was cordial, bordering on friendly, although I sensed that they had some concerns which they weren't sharing. I left them with "The Letter" and letters of reference. We ended the interview with Larry's saying he would call us over the weekend or next week. Apparently, there was another couple in Washington they were considering, but whom they had not yet met. Neither Sam nor I got our hopes up on this one, but you never knew. One thing I'd learned by now was that the quest for a baby was unpredictable. At the time we said goodbye to Shana and her parents, I did not know that in less than a week we would decide with whom we would cast our lot to have our child.

Chapter Seventeen

*A*t nine-thirty the next night, a woman named Claire called and left a message on our answering machine. I was at my office. After seeing the last of my patients, I retrieved the message remotely. The friendly, clear voice said that she saw our ad in the *Pennysaver* and would I please call her back. I wasted no time in returning her call. I learned that Claire was a twenty-six year old divorcée with four children who had been a surrogate mother five years before. Currently, she worked for an electronics firm. She said she had not been paid for being a surrogate, but did it as a favor to her childless friends. We talked for an hour on the phone. She sounded perky, bright, healthy, concerned, sensitive—and ideal. When I came home later that evening, I shared the content of our conversation with Sam. We decided to see her as soon as possible and I called back to make plans. We agreed to meet that Sunday morning at her home, one hundred and twenty miles from us in central Pennsylvania. Coincidentally, she lived five minutes away from Sandra, our only other surrogate mother candidate-of-the-moment. Despite our concerns about Sandra's intelligence, we arranged to meet both women on the same day—Sandra in her trailer and Claire in the home she owned. Although I was concerned about contracting with a single woman because of the risk of her changing her mind and deciding to keep the baby, we did not have many choices. A married couple, we reasoned, would be less inclined to keep another man's baby when they could have more, if

119

they wanted, by themselves. Of course, the success of a surrogate parenting arrangement depended wholly on the character of the parties involved. What we were looking for, really, was a reliable person, married or single. Despite her divorced status, Claire seemed to be the better candidate of the two. And Marla certainly thought a single woman's child would be easier for a single man to adopt.

That Sunday, we met with Claire and Sandra in two marathon back-to-back appointments. Both women, very different, lived within a mile of each other. Claire was first. Despite the long distance, we made great time driving and arrived in two hours. We ate breakfast at a local restaurant and arrived at eleven forty-five am Sunday morning, January nineteenth. Our visit lasted three and a half hours.

Claire MacKenzie was a twenty-eight year old divorced, overweight, pale, dark-haired, green-eyed mother of two daughters and two sons, ages two through nine. She had regular features and without the excessive weight (she weighed well over two hundred pounds), one would call her pretty. Her skin was smooth and clear and her dark hair looked like its owner made an effort to style it with a white band tied around her head. A former researcher, she now worked for a local electronics company. She grossed about $21,000 per year, owned her own home and had been divorced for two years.

She lived in a small, four-bedroom, white cedar-shingled, two story house in what appeared to be a working class neighborhood. Although the living room was neat, there were relatively few furnishings—a sofa, coffee table, recliner, console television and a few knick-knacks scattered about. We were welcomed with a smile and a handshake and encouraged to sit down. As we made ourselves comfortable, we began to scrutinize Claire for clues which might reflect her seriousness and reliability.

We found Claire to be a chatty, open, no-nonsense person with a good sense of humor. She answered all our questions frankly and sensed that we were "okay" people. As we became better acquainted, her engaging personality shone through, making her even more attractive.

At home that evening, Sam and I compared notes of the pros and cons of getting involved with Claire. On the positive side, she was bright (she had a college degree), independent—both emotionally and financially; mature; able to make long-range plans; had a higher risk for twins; didn't want more kids for herself; was willing to travel for doctor's appointments; had a history of easy pregnancies and childbirths; wanted our active involvement during the pregnancy; and, more than anything else, claimed to have done this before. She did not seem concerned about the money, couldn't even come up with a price, and indicated that her deceased father left her kids some money in a trust fund, which she planned on adding to with money she would make from being a surrogate mother. This she would use for her children's education.

On the negative side, she was less flexible about using a midwife than the other candidate, seemed naive and overeager to please, i.e., we got the impression that she gave us answers that she thought we might want to hear. In my opinion, she lacked depth in her thinking and seemed too ready to jump right into this after our first phone call only two days before. We also questioned her social support system as she had no significant other. By the end of our interview, we were exhausted, but guardedly optimistic.

From Claire's, we went directly to Sandra's, where she lived with her boyfriend and three children in a trailer owned by her boyfriend, Don. The drive took all of five minutes. As we pulled up to the trailer, which was parked along a dirt road in a rather run-down trailer park, we were greeted by Sandra and Don at their front door. The steps leading up to the trailer were rickety and we were cautioned to be careful in mounting them. Three young children were playing on the floor of the small living room.

We were exhausted from our previous session. Although unspoken, I sensed that neither of us had the energy for another three-hour marathon. The meeting got off to a slow start. Sandra and Don were relatively shy. Sandra was a pretty girl, with half her medium brown hair tied in back in a kind of pony tail and half of it coming down to her shoulders on both sides. She had bright blue eyes and a pretty smile. She was more responsive than assertive and seemed to find it difficult to initiate conversation. She was cooperative and answered our questions as fully as she could. There was, however, little embellishment, so the pace was halting. Her intellect was clearly inferior to Claire's.

Early in the interview, Sandra asked me, "Do you want to hold Dusty?" That was her youngest. I said, "Sure, I'd be happy to." As I took the little boy into my lap, I had flashbacks of the time with Kathy last summer, when I held her son and pretended, for a few minutes, that he was ours. I guessed this was her test to see how we'd be with babies. She asked me at the end, "Are you sure this is want you want full time—kids climbing all over, non-stop?" I said, looking straight into her eyes, "Absolutely." I told her that when we felt overwhelmed, we would play "tag-team" and say, "here, you take over." She confirmed that's what she and Don did.

When it came time to say goodbye, Sam's and my intuition told us that Sandra could be a successful surrogate mother. It was up to us to decide if we wanted her. Neither Sandra nor Don expressed concern about our being a male couple. Like Kathy's husband last year, Don said that he thought a child would be lucky to have two doctors for parents. We drove the long trip home discussing our impressions of each woman, hopeful that perhaps one of them would turn out to be the right one. My hopes were buoyed again.

Over the days that followed our meeting with Claire, we studied her application. The personality tests I had administered looked good and her responses to our questionnaire were consistent with what she had told us in our interview. She seemed to be a healthy, if somewhat guarded woman, calm, relaxed, and generally free of worry. Her test results suggested she seldom got angry at others and rarely experienced lasting feelings of sadness or depression. She claimed to be good at controlling her impulses (although the MMPI results contradicted this, suggesting that she preferred action to thought) and was quite confident about her ability to cope with stress. Her personality could be described as assertive, forceful and dominant. People like Claire enjoy large and noisy crowds or parties and prefer to be group leaders rather than followers. "Excitement, stimulation, and thrills have great appeal to her," a computer-generated report indicated. She was also described as "open" in style and high in aesthetic interests and as a person who enjoyed new and different activities. Surrogacy would certainly qualify in the "New and Different" category.

Each of the telephone conversations we had since our first meeting had been more positive and promising than the previous one. We had begun to build a trusting relationship with this person. After confirming her continued interest, Sam and I decided this was a serious candidate. We alerted the attorneys, the psychologist, and the obstetrician. We were setting our babymaking team into motion again.

The last possible hitch was our inability to contact the attorney who had handled her previous surrogacy. Initially, she was reluctant to divulge his name. Later, she said she would do so. We scheduled her formal evaluation with the psychologist for Thursday and her attorney's and obstetrician's appointments on Friday. We were rushing as Claire indicated that her "fertile" period was coming next week and that she wanted to get pregnant in January so that she would have the baby before the Thanksgiving and Christmas holidays. She didn't want the birth to interfere with her family life during the holidays.

This was incredible; in three days we should know whether we had a birthmother or not and in seven days she might be pregnant! Starting today, we would abstain from sex so our sperm count would be as high as possible. I didn't care if that was an old wives' tale— I wanted to do something to prepare for this event. It was too exciting to contemplate that if this insemination was successful, we could have a baby on my birthday, November seventh.

Since we decided to pursue Claire, I had become even more obsessed. I thought about getting pregnant constantly, just like I'd done with all the other surrogate and birthmother candidates. I was truly in a state of distraction.

By the last day of January, things really began to heat up. The day before, Claire had been interviewed by the psychologist in our home. The next day, she went for interviews with Nellie, the lawyer, and Dr. Shelly, the obstetrician. For today's appointments, we invited Claire to stay at our home overnight. It was quite an experience, having this stranger who wanted to bear us a child as a house guest. We were all on our best behavior.

Sam had arrived home before I did that night and started dinner. It was an awkward, yet amusing picture of 90's-style domestic life: me making a salad, Claire chopping an onion at the breakfast bar and Sam creating a wonderful Mexican casserole. As the three of us tossed, chopped, and folded, I thought about the symbolism of making a meal together. We were also going to make a baby together. Claire opened up a bit more, as did we, and we began our friendship over guacamole and enchiladas.

Before we sat down to dinner, I retreated to the bedroom to get the psychologist's report of her interview with Claire from the day before. Dr. Linda Deame did not like Claire, just as Claire said she hadn't liked Dr. Deame. The doctor thought we could not trust Claire. She doubted much of what Claire said, for example, Claire's saying she loses rather than gains weight during her pregnancies, or that she breast fed her youngest for three years. I hung up feeling depressed, wondering who this stranger was in our home. It didn't occur to me to challenge the psychologist's impression. Regaining my composure, I rejoined Sam and Claire for our meal, not mentioning the call and my inner turmoil.

After dinner, I asked Claire about her previous surrogacy. Her reaction made it clear that this was a sensitive subject. Claire put her foot down and told us she would not reveal the names of the people for whom she was a surrogate nor any information about the birth of the child or children. She even refused to tell us the name of her attorney so that we could verify her story.

We were concerned. Her credibility had already been called into question. We explained how important it was for us to have complete information in order to commit ourselves to her; that if she felt uncomfortable with our talking with that attorney, our lawyer could talk to him or her instead. All we wanted to do was to verify that it happened. She was adamant in her refusal.

It was after midnight by the time we finished dinner. As we continued to talk, Claire back-pedaled. She told us that her previous surrogacy was informal and that she had not been represented by counsel. She said that she lied to her obstetrician at the time by telling him that she was using her friend as a sperm donor so that she and her husband could have another child. She claimed she didn't want to tell her doctor she was being a surrogate mother. As the pregnancy progressed, she discovered she was going to have twins. The couple, however, only wanted to have one child. Claire became upset and the relationship deteriorated. Then, they abandoned her. They stopped coming to her prenatal doctor's appointments. They weren't in the delivery room with her at the birth. When she recovered, she left the hospital without the children and had to call the Department of Social Services to intervene. Eventually the couple adopted both children.

The story sounded made up. We didn't know what was truth and what was fiction. Why did these educated people not foresee that twins could occur and address it before it became a problem? Why would they abandon Claire, who was prepared to give them the greatest gift of all? Why was she so defensive about revealing their names, if her story was true? What was she hiding? Why had she said there was a lawyer involved when there wasn't? She said in our first meeting that she had been through an evaluation process, including psychological testing. Now she denied it. How could we trust Claire with these crucial questions unanswered?

We went to sleep that night feeling depressed, thinking that our relationship was disintegrating. Claire would not reveal important information which went straight to the issue of her credibility. We were reluctant to get involved with someone about whom we were now so doubtful. Further, Claire began applying pressure, saying that she would undergo artificial insemination on Wednesday but that if it was not successful, or that if we wanted to wait, she would not do it for at least three months because she did not want to be nine months pregnant during the Christmas holidays. All of our close friends and our lawyer asked why she was in such a hurry. Why did she want to do this so quickly? The nagging questions were disturbing. The last thing we had done before saying goodnight to Claire was to take samples of Claire's blood—for an HIV test, a pregnancy test, and syphilis test. Sam's lab would analyze them in the morning. Despite our concerns, we were desperate. We had to continue pursuing Claire.

The next morning was a Friday, the last day of January. Claire met with attorney Nellie for an hour. Then, she was evaluated by Dr. Shelly. Both liked her, thought she was a good candidate, and saw no reason not to go forward with the artificial insemination. The only one who was negative in her estimation was the psychologist. Even Dr. Deame said that despite the possibility of a personality disorder, she could not say for certain that Claire couldn't relinquish her baby. She might be difficult, the doctor opined, but she believed that Claire didn't want another baby.

Claire called me twice during the day; once after her appointment with Shelly and once after getting back home. She told me she liked and wanted to retain both the obstetrician and the lawyer we had chosen for her. Shelly found she had an infection, and put her on medication. He reassured her that it would not interfere with her chances of getting pregnant. By her account of her history to him, he also agreed she would ovulate next Wednesday.

The second time Claire called, she spoke with Sam. They laughed and seemed to have a good conversation. She was, as were we, planning on going ahead with the insemination on Wednesday, February fifth. Claire said she wanted us in the room during the insemination. I made an appointment for a sperm concentration for five-thirty p.m. at the lab near Shelly's office. If all went as planned, our ejaculate would be spun down to a small pellet, reconstituted with sterile solution and placed on Claire's cervix within an hour of producing it.

Our plan was to meet at the doctor's office at six p.m., sign the contract, do the insemination, say some prayers, then go out to dinner and the theater with Claire. We were excited at making an event of it and everyone was positive and hopeful that we finally had a match.

Chapter Eighteen

The weekend before the artificial insemination, we went for an overnight visit to the West Virginia hideaway of two old friends. With our dog in the back seat, we left early Saturday morning and enjoyed the feeling of getting away which only a long car trip can evoke. When we finally arrived, we had time for a hike in the woods before helping to prepare dinner. Stimulating conversation with friends over a great home cooked meal was one of my favorite pastimes. When we went to bed, we were grateful to be distracted from the anxiety of waiting for I-Day to arrive .

The telephone echoed through the house at four a.m. It was the lab calling Sam with stat results on one of Sam's patients. "By the way, Dr. Westrick, we have the results from Ms. MacKenzie's blood tests—do you want them?" Sam grunted his assent, more asleep than awake. The voice on the line said, "All test results are negative except one. Ms. Mackenzie is pregnant."

Sam was stunned. He came back into the bedroom and told me the news. It was as if a bomb had dropped. I felt disoriented. I couldn't believe that Claire—who insisted that she must undergo artificial insemination on Wednesday—was already pregnant. I leapt to conclusions. I thought I knew what she was trying to do. In my shock, I surmised that she knew she was already pregnant, found our surrogacy ad, and tried to capitalize on her accident by passing someone else's baby off as ours. I was enraged. Sam was more forgiving. He called the lab the next morning to find out what the possibilities were of a false positive. He found out that only some kind of uterine cancer—highly unlikely in Claire's case—could account for a positive result.

Finally, we resigned ourselves to accepting that she was a liar; that every story she told us that was unsubstantiated was suspect. We disqualified her. We called Marla and asked her to call Nellie and have her stop work and explain why. Both women were astounded; everyone felt betrayed. When we came home, Sam called Claire to tell her the results. There was no answer and Sam said he'd try again later. Sam called Dr. Shelly to tell him. Shelly, too, was floored. She even fooled her obstetrician.

Then Nellie called, saying she had Claire on the other line. Did we want to have a three-way conversation? I agreed, struggling to retain my composure. Claire denied knowing she was pregnant; she said she had two normal periods since her last intercourse and was as stunned as we were. The next morning, in a subsequent conversation about exactly when her last period was, she changed her story. At first she said it was before Christmas, then she said it was on New Year's Day. I didn't know what to believe.

Now we faced a big dilemma. Claire had to decide what to do about the baby. We knew she was against abortion. She had to decide whether to give it up for adoption or to keep it. If she wanted to give it up, we were prime candidates to adopt because we'd already established a relationship with her. What about the birthfather? Would he acknowledge paternity? Would she lie about him and present us with a confederate to act the part? Would the birthfather want to relinquish his parental rights to a gay couple? She said he was older and married, with grown children of his own. She could not imagine that he would want this child. It didn't take us long to acknowledge that all we really wanted was a child, no matter how he or she came to us.

We spoke again the next evening. Claire said she had gone to her family doctor that day to have the pregnancy test repeated. It was confirmed. As if two positive tests were not enough proof, she reconfirmed it at a public health clinic. Whatever the truth, I made it clear to Claire and Nellie that we were definitely interested in adopting this baby if she decided not to keep it. We both acknowledged that there was something providential about the circumstances under which we met and the turn our relationship had taken. Perhaps this had all been predestined.

Of all that was so unclear—who was Claire; who was the birthfather; would Claire carry this baby to term—one thing was perfectly obvious: if all went as nature intended, this woman would have a baby in approximately thirty-two weeks. It was nerve-wracking to anticipate having a relationship for the next eight months with someone whom we didn't yet trust.

Then, Claire called and asked if we really wanted to adopt this baby. I said, "Are you kidding? Absolutely!" Sam felt more hesitant, distrustful. He asked me, "Whatever happened to your anger?" I said, "I got it all out! If Claire's going to give up this baby, maybe we were meant to be its parents."

Interrupting this drama, I received two calls from a lawyer who read our ad in the *Pennysaver*. He said he was working with a Russian lawyer who knew of a baby up for adoption. He wanted fifteen thousand dollars. God, there were so many people out there looking to capitalize on people's desperation to have children. I was too distracted and distrustful to pursue it.

Two days later I wrote letters to our and Claire's attorneys to say thank you and goodbye. I talked with Claire about using an adoption agency to assist us instead of private attorneys. She was willing to do anything that we wanted to accomplish our mutual goal. I determined that the advantages of using an agency were numerous. Our relationship would be less adversarial: rather than speaking to each other through our attorneys, like opponents, one agency would represent both our mutual interests. Although the cost would be higher, adopting from a District of Columbia agency would have the advantage of being subject to the District's non-discrimination law which included protection from discrimination based on sexual orientation. Our attorney believed that Washington had a more tolerant, enlightened court than Baltimore County when it came to social issues such as adoptions by gay people. The Washington D.C. agency also looked appealing as I was still smarting from the recent defeat we suffered in our attempt to protect gays from discrimination with an amendment to the civil rights law in my county.

Less than a week after we decided to commit to adopting

Claire's baby, we got a call from Rabbi Solomon, an old friend of mine, about a biracial couple in his congregation who were pregnant and wanted to give the baby up for adoption. Having been asked to locate a suitable adoptive home for the baby, Rabbi Solomon thought of us as we had told him about our desire to adopt the previous fall. Ironically, we had already considered adopting a biracial baby but we had decided against doing so. Secondly, the rabbi indicated there was mental illness in the family. The proposal aroused a terrible conflict as we wanted a child so badly. Rejecting any prospect was difficult. However, we were also aware of the difficulties interracial kids faced and we feared that the racial difference, in addition to the sexual orientation difference of our family, might create unnecessary hardships. We asked to meet to discuss his proposal further, despite our commitment to Claire. Our past disappointments taught us to consider every option. In the back of my mind I felt doubtful that we would pursue this option.

Feeling a bit guilty, Sam and I met with Rabbi Solomon at Sam's office. It was good to see him after so long. I'd known him for twenty years. It was valuable to hear him share his knowledge about biracial families; his adopted daughter was African-American. We discussed his congregant's desire to find an adoptive home for their baby. We were terribly ambivalent about this. We wanted a baby more than anything—but one that looked kind of like us. We feared the effects of racism on such a child. We were flattered that he chose to approach us first. At the end of our meeting, we decided we would take a month to decide. We felt we could take the time because the woman was only about four and a half months pregnant.

Our first obstetrical appointment with Claire was scheduled for the next Wednesday. I was nervous—having so little trust in her and having been emotionally bruised so many times before. Common sense demanded that we keep looking for other candidates. Our adoption ad was coming out in the *Pennysaver* again. Maybe we'd find more candidates. Our lawyer thought that we should keep Claire as our ace in the hole but continue to pursue other avenues simultaneously. I guess that's why God created lawyers.

Claire called that night and again the next morning. She stayed home from work because she felt nauseated. This was the third week in a row in which she stayed home for a day. I wondered how long she could keep that up without getting fired. She said she was planning on applying to a program that gave food to single mothers. I wondered if she was planning to leave work and go on welfare. She was making noise about doing that, mainly because she was unhappy being transferred to the secretarial pool—purportedly because she was pregnant and her employer didn't want to risk damage to the fetus by ambient microwaves at work. She continued to say things I found hard to believe.

In our conversation, which was very friendly and lasted over an hour, she said she talked to Nellie on the phone and terminated their relationship as requested by us. She said Nellie was favorably inclined to our using an agency as that was how she and her husband adopted their son. Claire also talked frankly about her marriage and divorce. She described the marriage as terrible and indicated that she had to pay him alimony when it ended. She said she grew stronger as a result of the divorce and was now convinced that if she could go through that she could survive anything.

Finally, we talked about her strategy for telling her family about the pregnancy. She said she would tell her parents she "got in trouble;" had approached a Baltimore lawyer who found an adoptive couple; and would be going through an agency to accomplish the final adoption. If her sister backed her on this, as she thought she would, Claire felt confident that her parents would support her as well. She made it sound easy.

When I asked, Claire said she didn't know exactly what her mother did for a living. How could she expect me to believe that? I found myself getting angry when she said things that made me believe she was dissembling. Rather than confronting her, however, I dealt with it by entering my doubts into my journal. This helped me to ventilate the frustration I felt, but did not risk upsetting the relationship. The feeling of talking to someone whom one suspects to be unreliable is difficult to describe—similar to the way an ambassador might feel talking to the enemy's ambassador. These early conversations were so stilted. But while I so often doubted the veracity of her statements, I was also trying to form a relationship with her. After all, she was planning on being the mother of my child. For that, I wanted to love her and like her; but because of the misrepresentations I suspected I distrusted and feared her. Such completely opposing feelings co-existing at the same time made our relationship interesting, if stressful. We arranged to meet at the doctor's office the next Wednesday at six p.m.. As the months unfolded, Wednesdays would become our lucky days, the days we would mark off our calendar each week on our journey to Simon.

Chapter Nineteen

Wednesday, February nineteenth, was the date of our first prenatal appointment with Dr. Shelly. Claire arrived promptly with her four year old son in tow. She seemed nervous and withdrawn. In fact, she was downright chilly. I thought she'd changed her mind. After saying hello, she picked up a magazine and started reading. I was perplexed by her silence. Why wasn't she even making an attempt at conversation with us? Maybe she was as nervous as we were. I was heartened when she asked us to accompany her into the examining room.

Our friendship with Shelly and his psychiatrist-wife went back ten years. Shelly and Sam trained at the same hospital in different departments and years. We respected him highly and felt a great deal of affection for him. He understood our desire for a child. A strapping middle-aged man with a young man's smile, Shelly was tall, hirsute, and perpetually in need of a shave. He usually looked exhausted. He had an interpersonal sensitivity rare in surgeons. We felt lucky to have him as a friend and as the doctor who would deliver our baby.

We were also grateful that Claire would make the long journey for each of the regular appointments. For her, the distance helped to separate her pregnancy from her day-to-day life in an extremely small town. She would have dreaded going to the local doctor and knowing everyone in his waiting room. She didn't want to have to answer the uncomfortable questions posed by inquisitive neighbors.

Shelly asked Claire many questions about her obstetrical history. She said that the fetus' father knew of her decision to give it up for adoption and that he would relinquish his parental rights, too. She confided in me that she had told him that she was further along in gestation than was actually the case so he wouldn't pressure her to have an abortion. Before we left, Shelly prescribed prenatal vitamins and a sonogram to find out exactly when she had conceived so we would know the due date. He also recommended reading *What to Expect When You're Expecting*, by Arlene Eisenberg, et al. (Workman, 1991), a very helpful guide to pregnancy.

We had dinner together afterwards, something which became a tradition we continued throughout the pregnancy. Although the evening was a bit strained, we tried to enjoy ourselves. It was hard for me to enjoy Claire completely because I continued to feel distrustful. Sam later told me he felt uncomfortable getting closer to her than we had to—at least until we felt we could trust her. I agreed. At eleven that night, Claire called to let us know she got home safely. I appreciated her consideration.

It was going to be a difficult eight months. The estimated due date was October first. Claire was convinced it was going to be a girl. This jolted me into reality. All along I had assumed my first born would be a boy. Now I had to consider the possibility she might be a girl. Superficially, I thought that babies are all alike—if we could care for a boy we could care for a girl. Underneath, however, I was afraid I might not know how to properly care for a daughter when she got older. Boy or girl, I was determined to take the baby into my heart and into my home. I just didn't know how I was going to live with not knowing if we were going to be Dads at all. The next appointment was to be in five weeks.

A few nights later, Claire called to tell us when her sonogram and blood-work appointments were scheduled. She also said that she had some pictures of the biological father to show us that were taken on a trip to a park last summer. She said he had bright red hair, blue-green eyes, was Caucasian, and handsome. As great as that sounded, I wondered if I could believe her. Claire could show us pictures of any man and say that he was the birthfather.

She also said something she was to repeat later: we had to

consider whether we wanted more children, because she was thinking of having her tubes tied after this one was born. If we wanted more down the line, she said she'd be willing to have another child for us. It sounded too good to be true. She hadn't even had one for us yet, and she was talking about having another. Her sentiments, however altruistic, had an idealistic ring to them, an innocence that I found disconcerting. It seemed that almost every interaction with Claire generated more ambivalence in me—happiness that she appeared to be responsible and considerate, worry because I doubted her stories.

The night after she had her sonogram, Claire called again with delight in her voice. "I have two pictures of your baby. I'll mail them to you." She was surprised to learn that they're now doing both trans-abdominal as well as trans-vaginal sonograms (she had both). She said the technician, a woman, was very nice and showed her a lot, including little limb buds (which she said moved in response to jiggling the uterus), the brain, eyes, heart and spine. She also said the technician knew her obstetrician and was surprised she was having her prenatal care so far away. Claire managed to avoid an explanation.

Claire talked a great deal about the cost of having a baby. She had never had to pay for prenatal care before. She was shocked by the mounting bills, even though her insurance paid the majority of the cost and we paid only the small co-payments. I was touched that she felt concerned about the financial expense her pregnancy caused us, even though it seemed a small price to pay for us.

She planned to talk to her parents about the pregnancy and adoption soon. She thought it would be hard. She said her mother could be mean and hateful. Could she be projecting? I hoped her mother wouldn't try to convince Claire to keep the baby. Claire saw this as a kind of showdown with Mom. She didn't anticipate having as much difficulty with her father. She believed he would support whatever decision she made.

She promised that she would bring pictures of the birthfather to our next doctor's appointment since she had "forgotten" the last time. She also confirmed that she had a babysitter for her children for two weeks prior to the delivery. We arranged for her to stay with us for the last two weeks of her pregnancy. Although I was a little apprehensive about an extended visit, I believed it would be worse with her so far away from us, her doctor, and the hospital where she was planning to deliver so close to her due date. And I shuddered when I thought of her driving the one hundred fifteen miles in labor.

She talked for the better part of an hour. She seemed to need to have contact with us. I wanted to believe she was trying to share the pregnancy experience, but I wondered with all this contact before the baby came, would she be able to separate from us as well as the baby after the birth? I made a sincere effort to offer unconditional support to Claire throughout these months and dealt with my own questions and insecurity internally and with Sam.

Three days later, the envelope from Claire arrived. It was a greeting card with a picture on the cover of a bunny in a praying position. Inside, it read:

I'm so thankful for the blessing of your friendship.
Love, Claire.

Inserted in the card were two polaroid sonogram photographs. One seemed to be a close-up, with the baby larger, but fuzzier. In the other, the baby appeared to be more in focus, but smaller. In both, I could see a tiny embryo, nine weeks old, a creature which looked more like a tadpole than a human being. Limb buds, large eyes, a curving spine, brain—all the signs of the beginnings of life. These were my first pictures of the baby. The photos were indescribably exciting and I was awestruck. My joy, so hard to contain, was tainted with the fear of abandonment. When was I going to get over this insecurity?

Chapter Twenty

*I*n her tenth week I retrieved a phone message on our machine. "Pray for me, I'm bleeding. I'm going to the hospital," Claire's frightened voice told our tape. Terrified, I called her back. She had just returned from the emergency room. She explained that she had abdominal pain and light bleeding early that morning and was afraid she might be miscarrying. After being examined, she was told that it did not appear to be a miscarriage, that she should go home, stay in bed, call her doctor in the morning, and go back to the hospital if the bleeding or abdominal pain worsened. I couldn't get in touch with Shelly, but the doctor covering for him said there was nothing more that could be done that night.

I called Claire the next morning. There was no answer. Nor was she at work. Either she was on her way to Shelly's office or back in the hospital. I prayed she wasn't miscarrying. Later I learned that she had left to take her children to school. She called me after having spoken to Shelly. He said she was okay and should continue to have bed rest. He believed her nausea may have caused strain which resulted in the bleeding, but that the baby was most probably fine. A second sonogram he had ordered revealed the yolk had been absorbed, a good sign, and there was good umbilical attachment.

On March eighth, Claire called to thank me for the book list I had sent from the Child Welfare League. Previously, she had asked about literature which addressed the concerns of children whose mothers planned to give siblings up for adoption. Apparently, the older and younger ones took the news well, but a middle child was unhappy, crying a lot but not talking about his feelings. Claire suspected this little boy didn't want his Mommy to give away his baby brother or sister. Claire was her usual chatty self and the call lasted almost three hours. She discussed her kids' feelings about the intended adoption, as well as her own feelings and those of her boyfriend. She expressed her strongest intent to carry out the relinquishment and said that she had neither the time nor the inclination for another child in her family. She also reaffirmed her boyfriend's intent to relinquish his parental rights and let her be in control of this adoption. She expressed confidence in our ability not only to parent the child, but to relay to the child at an appropriate age that his mother relinquished him based on love and concern for the child's welfare. She told me about her dream in which she was reminded of the movie, "Three Men and A Baby." She laughed as she recalled a fragment of the dream in which we were tying a young girl's hair in pig-tails and got them off center. She said she would give the child a locket her grandmother gave her if it was a girl and something else if it was a boy.

She said her mother had come over last week, feeling hurt—not that Claire was giving up the baby but that she didn't call her to ask if she would stay with the children while Claire was in Baltimore having the baby. As if she could read my insecurity when she mentioned her mother, Claire assured me that her mother would not want to take this baby and raise it. It was a positive conversation. Claire acknowledged that she would be in a great deal of pain at the time of the birth and cry a lot, but that she would ultimately stick to her intent to relinquish, despite knowing that a part of her would feel as if one of her children was dying. I was impressed by her acknowledgment of her ambivalence over this adoption and heartened that maybe we would really succeed in adopting this baby. Claire also told me that her decision would not be affected by the sex of the baby. I, too, reiterated that we would accept with love and gratitude whatever child we received. I was beginning to trust her.

Three days later, we rolled into the eleventh week. Claire called on Saturday and told me that she could feel the baby inside her—it felt like having butterflies in her stomach. She couldn't feel it outside yet, but she could feel it moving inside. She told me that she bought some maternity clothes. She also shared with me that she had told her sister all about her intention to give up the baby for adoption to a gay couple, something she said she hadn't told anyone. Rather than confront her, I accepted it, even though we had agreed she was not to tell anyone about us for fear it might jeopardize the adoption. She said her sister was comfortable with it, as long as Claire was. All that the rest of the family knew was that the couple are two doctors, a psychologist and a family practitioner. Interestingly, she said she met with her attorney last Wednesday to rewrite her will. Specifically, she had him draft a letter of intent to certify that she wanted us as guardians of the baby after it is born. She did not want any confusion in case she died or became incapacitated. That way, no one in her family would become burdened by this baby and we would be assured of having custody. This action, unsolicited on our part, was greatly reassuring. It spoke to her intent of not keeping the baby. Every day my confidence in this amazing, vexatious woman grew and my doubts faded.

Finally, we talked a fair bit about homosexuality. She asked, "How do you know if someone is gay if they're not real obvious?" Then, "Do people think of you as their "gay" friends as opposed to just Ken and Sam?" She was genuinely interested in learning about our lifestyle, but also puzzled by why our gayness didn't bother her more. She thought most people might be bothered by a gay couple adopting an infant. I appreciated her candor and appreciated her questions as natural expressions of her curiosity.

We next spoke about a week later. In a calm voice she said her middle child woke her up at two a.m. covered with red spots. Claire was covered with them, too. She said her mother thought it was measles. I started "terriblizing"—a word I used with patients in therapy who anticipated unrealistically catastrophic consequences of problems in living. What was in store for our baby? Blindness? Birth defects? Therapeutic abortion? I called Sam right away. Claire said she was unable to see her doctor, who was on vacation; she wanted to see if I could get in touch with the doctor covering for him. Sam gave me a list of questions to ask Claire. Her answers gave me hope that she wasn't really sick with German measles. Has she had measles in the past? (Yes) What kind? (German, she thinks). She's also had chicken pox, and mumps, but not scarlet fever. She said the oldest child was immunized with measles-mumps-rubella vaccine but the younger ones were not. She was not on medication and she could not think of what she and her daughter might be having an allergic reaction to. Also, she did not describe any of the flu-like symptoms usually found before the onset of German measles. She agreed to try to see her family doctor that day. Sam thought it was suspicious that she was perfectly fine when we spoke last night and "covered from head to toe" today. As it turned out, the diagnosis was an allergic reaction. The baby was fine and so would be the mother. No one had German measles.

When Week Thirteen came, I woke up before Sam that Saturday morning feeling depressed—another day of being child-less. My despair felt so deep, so palpable. Until we had this child, I feared I would continue to have a low-grade depression, like a wound which never quite healed. More and more, I appreciated the pain of infertility, a feeling one rarely associates with men. On Wednesday we were going to have our second visit with Dr. Shelly and Claire. I hoped that we would be able to see a sonogram again, so we could see how the baby had grown. Shelly had been a prince thus far. Again, I thought how lucky we were to have this old friend participating so intimately in the creation of our family.

We planned, as before, to go out to dinner afterwards. Having made this a ritual enabled us to get better acquainted with our birthmother. After our recent rubella scare, I hoped that things would be quieter. I couldn't believe that we were close to the end of the first trimester already. My life seemed to revolve around our doctor's appointments. Everything between them—my patients, our friends, family, travel plans, was so much "filler"—things to do which took up time until the next really meaningful thing came along—a visit with the obstetrician. Every visit brought us a step closer to Simon.

I wished that I could experience the joy of the typical expect-ant father. He could boast and brag and prepare. In adoption, there are no guarantees. At any time we could lose this baby—through miscarriage, abortion, deception or caprice. Claire could change her mind about adoption or about us at any time—as could the baby's biological father. Even after we take the baby home we could lose him. I felt sorry for myself—the alternating joy and terror of this pregnancy. My friend, Lance, encouraged me not to suppress my joy in expecting the baby. Rather, he advised, feel it for all its fullness. If I am to be disappointed, it will hurt whether I've been happily expecting the baby or quietly hoping for it.

The second visit took place on the day the baby was fourteen weeks in gestational age. Sam and I arrived ten minutes early. We didn't recognize the lone figure in a red striped top and red pants in the waiting room at first. It was Claire in a new hairdo. I was a bit shocked that I didn't recognize her instantly, this object of my fascination and the mother of our child-to-be. I'd talked with her so often. It reminded me that I had become more intimate with her as a voice on the phone than as a personal friend. It was her voice that was so familiar, not her face.

She was reading her local paper, a thin affair she likened to a gossip column. She had been waiting an hour because the new route she used got her there faster than the former route she had driven. She was significantly warmer than in our first meeting last month. We chatted idly before she handed me a letter, properly notarized, that she said her lawyer had drafted. I smiled inwardly as I read the document with a notary's raised seal:

CONSENT OF PARENT FOR
THE ADOPTION OF A MINOR

I, Claire MacKenzie, am the mother of a child to be born in September. After full deliberation and consideration, I have decided that the best interests of my child will be served if he/she is adopted by Dr. Kenneth Morgen. Therefore, I give my consent to his adoption of my child.

_____

Signature

One would have thought that I would be ecstatic. At last, concrete proof that we were getting this baby. But, again, I experienced a feeling of unreality. The last time a pregnant woman gave me "proof" that she was going to give us her baby was last Thanksgiving when Sandy gave us that little blue shopping bag with a child's toy and a card addressed to "Mommy and Daddy" inside. I had the same feeling of dread then, that this was fate's cruel joke; that it didn't mean anything. Claire could still change her mind at any time and keep or take back this baby. I wish the letter could have comforted me, as I'm sure it was intended to do, but it mostly made me feel uneasy. It was so hard to be empathetic and supportive of Claire when I felt so vulnerable.

While we waited for Shelly, Claire told us that her priest recommended that she go into counseling. She told us she had one visit at the local counseling center with a social worker, who told her she was arrogant. I knew she should have counseling, for her sake and for ours, but I was afraid when she told me she had gone. I thought that she would best be served by an open-minded (non-homophobic) counselor, something that's hard to screen out when searching for a therapist. I told her that the best counselors were neutral about adoption but some had personal opinions about it which could affect a birthmother's decision-making ability. I was particularly concerned about how she would deal with the issue of the sexual orientation of the prospective adoptive parents. I feared that in that small, Catholic town, it might undo our efforts if it was disclosed.

Finally, the nurse called Claire back to weigh her and put the Doppler stethoscope over her uterus to get the fetal heartbeat. We started to accompany her but Claire indicated she usually was seen alone at the beginning of the visit—a comment which mystified us. It only took five minutes for Shelly to come to us in the waiting room and ask if we wanted to look at the sonogram again. I was eager to do it and said yes, although Sam was restrained. He told me later that Shelly had questioned whether it was wise to encourage Claire to have sonograms each visit as that might further attach her to the baby and make the relinquishment she intended more difficult. Claire, however, was eager to show off and educate us and I was happy to learn. With the lights out, we saw a tiny blip on the video monitor. I was barely able to make out any details. It was hard to appreciate that this was my son or daughter. The heart was a throbbing shadow on the screen, beating so fast, I was afraid it would burst. The umbilicus was also prominent, but no features were visible. I continued to have a feeling of disbelief, unreality. I couldn't feel the good feelings other expectant fathers must have when they see their babies so long before they are born. Our paternity was too tentative. I guess the good feelings must wait. They will come when the baby comes—and Claire goes.

Next, Claire offered to let us hear the baby's heartbeat through the Doppler stethoscope. This was a contraption with a metal ball-bearing type microphone on one end connected by an electric cord to a small speaker. It reminded me of a pocket radio. Shelly was out of the room so Sam fetched it. When he started to get the conductive jelly, Claire stopped him and tried to get a heartbeat without using the jelly. She manipulated it around her belly, but was unable to hear anything. When Shelly returned, he applied the jelly and promptly found the heartbeat. It was quick—about one hundred eighty beats per minute—and sounded like a train rolling down the tracks.

After the appointment, there was no time to go over the records of Claire's previous pregnancies that we had sent for. I made a mental note to call Shelly the next day to get the low-down. He could not distinctly remember what, but he told Sam there were some inconsistencies in Claire's account of her history and that of the record. We had dinner together, as usual. Our dinners were becoming increasingly comfortable. We finished at eight-thirty p.m. and returned directly home, waving goodbye to Claire as we took our exit on the interstate. It would be eleven o'clock when she arrived home. I felt sorry for Claire, having such a long drive ahead of her at this time of night and prayed that she didn't get into a car accident.

The next morning, I called Claire and expressed my concern about the confidentiality of her psychological clinic setting. She said she had not told her counselor any specifics about us, other than to say that one was a family doctor and the other was a psychologist and that the child would be well cared-for. She said she would stick to that. We confirmed the dates of our upcoming vacation and I agreed to call her the day after our return. By that time, she would have had her alpha fetoprotein test to screen for birth defects and we would have had a needed vacation and family reunion.

Chapter
Twenty-One

Wednesday, April first was the beginning of Week Fourteen. April Fool's Day. Ten a.m. The phone rang—the baby line. I was outside having coffee and surveying the landscape. A timid voice identified herself as "Annie" and asked, "Did you place the ad for an adoption?" It was an old ad, but I said, "Yes," and went inside to get better reception on the portable phone. Annie described her situation, sounding teary and upset. "I've never made a call like this before," she confided. "I've been thinking about this for three months, since Ian was born."

This was a twist—a caller who had already given birth. Annie was thirty-three and had four children ranging in age from two months to fourteen years. They were all by different fathers and she had never been married. Ian was healthy but born two months premature and had to spend his first three weeks in the neonatal intensive care unit.

"I thought about getting an abortion," she said, "but I just couldn't—I'm Catholic. I just can't care for another child. Frank, Ian's father, is no help. I hate myself for depriving the other children of their childhoods." Annie was poor, worked as a cashier and was on Medical Assistance. Her boyfriend was in jail. She cried on the phone as she expressed her concern about robbing the childhoods of her older children because they were required to take care of the younger children. She felt that because of their poverty and the lack of paternal support it would be best to give the baby up. She said she hadn't done it sooner because she had been so ambivalent about this decision. This woman needs counseling, I thought.

Coincidentally, Annie's doctors, a married couple, were family practitioners who had trained in Sam's program and were acquaintances of ours. They had recently been to our home and were aware of our desire to adopt. Annie had confidence in them and, because they knew us, I believed they would be able to reassure her that we would be good adoptive parents.

I invited her to come over at three o'clock that afternoon. It was a beautiful, bright, but chilly spring day. She agreed, asking if she could bring the baby. I said, "Of course" and immediately after the call, I called Sam to tell him the exciting news and to make sure he was home by three. I called the adoption agency to get an update on what to do if she wanted to go through with it.

At three-thirty, an old black car pulled up to the back door. It was Annie. I went out to greet her along with our cat and dog. She commented absentmindedly about the niceness of our property but was obviously in emotional distress. In her arms was clutched a tiny bundle wrapped in a blue nylon baby suit. I welcomed her warmly. I ushered her into the living room and introduced her to Sam, who was already seated there. She was quick to ask if I wanted to hold Ian and handed me the baby right away. His hair was fine and red. His eyes were clear blue. His skin was white and he looked perfect. Absolutely perfect. But by now I had done this several times, and I suppressed my excitement. I rocked the baby and held him in my lap. When he started to cry, I gave him his pacifier and that seemed to quiet him down. It was wonderful to hold a baby in my arms even though I was working hard to keep myself from getting lost in the experience.

As we started discussing her story, Sam's presence made things awkward for Annie, who did not yet understand why he was there. Sam was upset that I had not told her over the phone that we were a male couple. After a few minutes of conversation, she asked where my wife was. What a tense, awkward moment. I looked right into her eyes and said, "Sam and I are the couple. I don't have a wife." I told her that I was referring to Sam when I said "we" had been together for fourteen years. I thought I saw a flash of anger in her eyes, but it quickly passed and she declared weakly, "I'm not prejudiced." She did have questions, however. "How can y'all mother a child? Would the child be gay? What about his friends; won't they tease him?"

We tried to answer each question with patience and understanding, but I'm not sure we convinced her. I explained that children needed "mothering ones," a term I did not tell her I borrowed from psychiatrist Harry Stack Sullivan who coined it earlier in the century. The mothering one was not necessarily the biological mother, but the parent who performed the nurturing functions to which Annie referred: feeding, holding, changing, comforting, etc. It could be the father, a grandparent, or a nanny. As doctors, Sam and I were nurturing by nature. We told Annie that we could do everything any mother could do to care for a child except breast feed.

As far as the child's sexual orientation was concerned, that was my area of my expertise, so I was comfortable in responding. First, I told Annie that there was no formula for creating sexual orientation—either homosexual or heterosexual. The overwhelming majority of homosexuals came from heterosexual homes, suggesting that role modeling was not a deciding factor. Research about children raised by homosexuals did not suggest a higher than normal incidence of homosexuality in the offspring. Further, even if the child would turn out to be gay, we would not consider that a bad outcome. We were living proof that gay people could lead happy, healthy and productive lives. If our child was gay, he could be happy too. I explained that research demonstrated no difference in mental health between gay and straight people.

I went on to explain to Annie that any child can be teased by his or her peers for things about that child that are different: skin or hair color, height, weight, socioeconomic status, etc. Some children are teased for the families they come from, e.g. immigrant, adoptive or divorced. We expect that our child might be teased for having two fathers and no mother. To minimize the ill effects of such teasing on our child we planned to instill in him a strong sense of confidence and self-esteem by raising him with love and affirmation. I told Annie that we would not place our child in an environment where he would be at risk for lack of support by those in authority. Sam and I would work closely with our child's school teachers and administrators to educate them about our family and how to handle such teasing affirmatively. We discussed the meaning of the word, "diversity," and how it applied to today's families. Further, I reminded her that our child would be raised by two highly educated people in a culturally and socio-economically advantaged home— one in which any child being raised would benefit. Finally, I told Annie about the gay and lesbian family play group that we were going to join. Our chapter, with sixty gay and lesbian families, would provide our child with the opportunity to make friends with other children from similar homes, thereby validating him and helping him to adjust to whatever sense of being different he might have. I told her I had even contemplated writing children's books for him because there was a dearth of appropriate material on the market.

Annie spent two hours with us—the time flew by. I was excited by the possibility that this could be it. Annie said she had an appointment with her doctor next week and she would talk it over with him. We felt good about that. Her doctors knew us and could vouch for us. We parted with the understanding that I would call her on Wednesday to find out the result of their meeting. I'd be making that call from Palm Springs, because we were to leave the next morning for our California vacation and family reunion.

Through all this, Claire's presence was in the foreground of my consciousness and I felt more than vaguely unfaithful. Somehow, I sensed that this prospective adoption was not going to work out. Despite our excitement, neither Sam nor I were convinced that adoption was in Annie's and her family's best interest. When I called her the next morning to get her address, a child answered the phone who seemed to be coached by a voice in the background, saying her mother wasn't there. Knowing that Annie was probably home but didn't want to speak to me, I told the child I wanted to send a letter to her mother and needed her address. The child put me on hold again, asked an adult for their address, and gave it to me. Sending her "The Letter" was the last thing I did before starting to pack for our trip the next day to the California desert and the warm embrace of Sam's loving family—now my extended family, too.

I thought more about my sense of being unfaithful to Claire. Claire seemed to be depending on us to adopt her child. Being seasoned, prospective adoptive parents, however, we appreciated that the plan could fall through at any time. Everyone had told us we had to keep our options open and not turn down any possibility. I believed that if we adopted Ian, any number of qualified, prospective adoptive parents would snatch up Claire's baby in a second. Even we might be ready for Claire's baby by September! Yet, I couldn't believe we might have a baby to adopt as soon as we returned from California. Even though Annie's appearance in our lives was fortunate, I could feel my stress levels go up.

Sam and I returned renewed from ten wonderful days in southern California. The weather was hot and sunny and we had our fill of basking in the sun, swimming, and playing on manicured golf courses. The effect the desert had on me was immediate. I ate more healthfully and exercised every day. But despite the great weather and fun reunion with the family, I found myself drifting back to the phone date I had on Wednesday with Annie. When the appointed hour finally came, she answered the phone, obviously still asleep. It was ten a.m. her time. She asked me to call back a little later, not a good sign. When I called back an hour later, she was alert and apologized for not being up when I called. Annie said she took Ian to the doctor but did not discuss adoption with him. Another bad sign. She said she was still mulling it over and had invited her mother to spend the weekend with her so they could talk it over alone. I knew she needed to discuss it with someone. She asked me to call her when we returned from California.

After we returned, I again called her at the agreed-upon time but there was no answer. I called again later and her boyfriend answered the phone. He said Annie was not home and asked who I was. I told him and asked if he would have her call me. He asked where I was from and I told him the call was personal. He insisted and I repeated that it was a personal call. When he then got nasty, I told him I'd call back. He said "fuck you" and we hung up. More bad signs. Annie had told me she was booting him out and obviously had not done so. I'd try again, but unless I heard from her I was not going to try too hard; there were too many red flags. I never heard from Annie again.

On a more positive note, I called Claire and found out she was starting to show. "My tummy is bigger than my bosom," she cooed. She also said she was going to counseling twice a month and reiterated that, although she anticipated having a hard time coming home from the hospital without a baby, she was not considering changing her mind. She sagaciously indicated that she knew she needed emotional support and that she thought we'd feel better knowing she had a professional therapist rather than her family to rely on—someone who could be non-judgmental and unbiased. She anticipated going weekly after the birth for a few sessions. Other-wise, she sounded perky, jealous that we had tans, and looking forward to our next meeting with the doctor in eight days.

She also said she was scheduled to have the alpha fetoprotein test on Saturday. I planned to call Shelly afterwards to find out the results of the test and to see if the records were received from her last pregnancy. I hoped there would be no more surprises.

For our third prenatal visit, in Week Seventeen, we arrived promptly at six p.m. at Shelly's office. Claire was sitting primly in the waiting room. It felt a bit more comfortable this time. I guess because of the lengthy telephone conversations we'd been having. Shelly looked particularly tired, having delivered a baby in the middle of the night.

Claire dutifully went to the bathroom to produce her urine sample in the cup before her examination, a ritual repeated monthly. The nurse invited me in to hear the baby's heartbeat through the Doppler stethoscope. The whooshing sound still reminded me of a powerful train leaving a station. Shelly measured the fundus (the top of the uterus, I learned) with a measuring tape by holding it between the top of her pubic hair and the bottom of her belly button. He told all of us that the baby was growing normally. He assured us that everything was proceeding just fine. He also noted that, just as she had predicted, Claire lost two pounds as opposed to gaining the four pounds that the textbooks predicted. Shelly hadn't yet received the records he had requested of the twin birth, so he had Claire fill out release forms again and sent them off to the previous doctor's office and the hospital where she said she had given birth. This absence of verification of her previous surrogacy was a dim, but constant source of worry.

At the appointment, I saw the sonogram report. The baby was due on September thirtieth. On February twenty-seventh it had a gestational age of approximately nine weeks and one day. Since gestational age was counted from the beginning of the last menstrual cycle prior to fertilization, the baby was most likely conceived on or about January eighth, not New Year's Eve. Since Claire would not have anticipated her period until January twenty-second and she first called me on January sixteenth, she could not have known she was pregnant at the time. That was a big relief and finally put to rest the question about her veracity on this topic. Although she may have wondered if she was pregnant, she could not have known she was pregnant at the time she first called me because her period was not due for another six days. Discovering this helped me finally to begin to trust Claire.

The next day I purchased, *What to Expect When You're Expecting*, the book Shelly so highly recommended. I also read some pamphlets at Shelly's office which explained the childbirth process and how to anticipate bringing home your baby. I had to prepare myself for what lay ahead.

Two weeks later, we were scheduled to go to Phoenix for four days. I was excited to be returning to a resort—the Phoenix Biltmore—for a medical conference with Sam. Although I was to address the conference on issues pertaining to the significant others of doctors who provided HIV care, I was along primarily for rest and relaxation. I was also looking forward to seeing Sam's sister and brother-in-law for golf and dinner on Saturday. They were vacationing there too, by coincidence. With all the tension of the pregnancy, it was going to be very nice to get away.

Three nights prior to leaving, Claire called and we talked at length. She again asked if we wanted to have another baby because if we didn't she would have her tubes tied. I was moved by her repeating this demonstration of good faith. I admitted to myself I was also wary. I was still having a problem trusting Claire completely.

Claire explained why she thought that it was okay for her to have a baby for two gay men. She felt that because there was no woman in the picture she would not be jealous. There would be no question of another woman taking her place or doing something for her (raising her child) that she could not or would not do for herself. She said this came out in her most recent counseling session. She seemed proud of her insight. She also acknowledged that she would never be a brain surgeon or make a major contribution to society. By placing her child in an advantaged home, she reasoned, she might be able to contribute to society vicariously by enabling her offspring to make such a contribution. She felt that Sam and I might be able to make it possible for her child to accomplish great things in life— things which would lend her own life more meaning.

She also admitted that she didn't tell us the whole story of the previous pregnancy. She reiterated that what she had told us was true—that she had twins, that she gave them up for adoption, and that it was a surrogate pregnancy. She said she'd tell us the whole story when she came to stay with us during the last weeks of the pregnancy. This was going to be interesting.

Further, she explained why she had procrastinated about telling us more about the birthfather. She was afraid that we might change our minds. I shuddered in fear that she was projecting on this one. That is, was she the one who might change her mind? I asked her, "Does he have two eyes, two ears, one nose and one mouth?" She said, "Yes." I said, "That and an average IQ was all he needed in my book." However, her reluctance to disclose information more fully about him made me wonder about what she was withholding and why. She seemed to think that withholding pertinent information would assure the success of the adoption. I had to find a way to tell her that while we would adopt her baby regardless of how it came out, we needed to know all relevant information and to have her provide full disclosure. Claire frightened me because at the same time we were building trust, she would say things that would cause me to question her trustworthiness.

I'd been counting down the weeks until the birth. We were at Week Eighteen, the second trimester, with exactly five and a half months to go. In nine weeks, on June first, we would begin the last trimester. The counting helped to ease the incredible excitement that was growing in the core of my being.

Chapter
Twenty-Two

We returned from the Phoenix conference on Sunday. The next Wednesday would mark Week Twenty—the halfway point in the pregnancy. In our last conversation, Claire had said she could feel the baby kicking inside. While away, we met a number of other gay doctor couples like us; two who both had infants by artificial insemination and one who was pregnant. More and more couples like us seem to be succeeding in building families. When I saw them holding their babies, I wanted to cry. I didn't dare hold the children for fear of breaking down. I noticed I was becoming more emotional as we got closer to the birth. What next? Was my belly going to swell up in sympathy?

As we got closer to the due date, Sam and I had to concentrate more on the logistics of the adoption. Would this be a single-parent or co-parent adoption? Recent precedent-setting cases of second-parent adoptions in D.C. suggested we might be able to proceed as a couple, but they were different from ours. Each of those couples included a biological parent and the other partner had already had, for some time, a parental relationship with the child. If we were to successfully attempt a co-parent adoption from birth, we would set a new precedent. If we were turned down, we could potentially lose the baby altogether. I discussed it with Marla who said she would consult with national experts at an upcoming conference about the merits of each approach. Nearly half-way home, we still were not sure exactly how we would accomplish this adoption. As if there wasn't enough to worry about, now I had something else to obsess over.

On May twelfth, Claire called, "Hi! Guess what day it is? It's the halfway mark—twenty weeks down, twenty weeks to go!" I was seated at my desk and glanced at the calendar. Sure enough, a big "20" was marked on the page. She said she could feel the baby kicking daily now—what the baby book called "quickening." We were counting down the weeks together. She predicted the baby would be born on September twenty-third—one week before the sonogram's predicted due date. She thanked me for the flowers I sent for Mother's Day and talked about how she spent the morning with her family.

Lately, I had been thinking about how to spend the time left before the baby's birth. Should we take a trip? How much should we prepare a nursery? I was still afraid that she might change her mind. I was haunted by memories of all of our failed adoption attempts. My friends had been congratulating me in odd ways. They knew the losses we had suffered and how much we wanted a baby. They knew that this could fall through at any time. They wanted to be supportive, but, like me, didn't want to be disappointed again. Their congratulations, their expressions of joy in anticipation of the birth were muted. I understood.

Psychologically, I'd been preparing myself for months, long before we'd known Claire. I had been thinking about how our lives would change forever; how my spare time would no longer be my own and how much less of it I would have. I thought about how becoming a father would mean a change in my identity from being a son, grandson and lover. In a way, becoming a father and accepting responsibility for another was the final stage of growing up. I was looking forward to, not afraid of these changes.

The next day, Claire called again, saying "I've been thinking of you and just called to say `hi.'" I told her I was thinking of her, too. In fact, I dreamed that morning of being in the examining room feeling her stomach while the baby was kicking. We talked at length about her kids, her family of origin, and her experiences growing up. Something in me was melting. I started opening up to her, too. We began drawing closer. After almost five months of acquaintance-ship, it was about time.

Finally, Claire revealed the real reason for her call. She told me that her relationship with the baby's father was over. She was upset. Apparently, he had told his wife about the affair and Claire's pregnancy. I asked her if that would jeopardize his commitment to the adoption and she said no. However, she said for the first time that she wanted to write "unknown" on the birth certificate in the space for the birthfather. She felt the baby was hers alone to give away. I became frightened again, wondering how secure this adoption would be if she misrepresented the paternity. Was Claire telling us the truth? Why wouldn't she give us his name? I asked her about speaking to him or having our lawyer speak to him but she felt the less he was involved the better. She indicated that the relationship was over and that she could only guarantee that he would sign documents at the time of the birth.

Claire said again that she was afraid that if we knew more about him we might not want to adopt their baby. I expressed my concern to her about excluding information which she felt might jeopardize our adopting. She finally seemed to believe that we were committed and said she'd bring pictures of the birthfather to our next appointment. She also said she would tell us about the past surrogacy over dinner after our next doctor's appointment. I asked her why we still had not received a picture of the birthfather. She didn't explain. She said she would try to remember them, but I feared she had changed her mind and would not bring them to the next appointment. I ended the conversation, worried about all the things that could go wrong, particularly about getting the father's permission. I was dismayed that she continued to promise to show us a picture of him and continued to forget to bring it. Our fourth prenatal visit was only five days away.

On May nineteenth, the night before that visit, Claire and I had another long conversation. I asked her if she loved the baby. She said that was not a fair question. Claire typically avoided discussing painful topics. I told her I thought she did love this baby but she never said so. I wondered about how she might react if he showed up on her doorstep in eighteen years. I told her that I learned in my adoption classes that adopted kids often search for their biological parents. Would Claire be receptive if the child wanted to meet her some day? She said, "yes." We acknowledged that we needed to talk about how she would like us to tell the baby about his birthmother when he asks.

We also talked about how she wanted things to be in the hospital. She said she wanted to be on the maternity ward and to get to visit with the baby. She would want some time alone with him to say goodbye. She talked for the first time about her ambivalence about wanting and not wanting to keep the baby. She said her counselor was going to be on call for her the week of the birth. She did not give me the impression that she was going to change her mind. She again promised to bring us a photograph of the baby's father. As the weeks passed, I gained increasing confidence that Claire would give us her baby. I was coming to realize that just as she was helping us, we were helping her. Just as we had difficulty trusting her, she had difficulty trusting us.

The appointment time arrived and we got to the waiting room about five minutes late. Claire was not there. She came about five or ten minutes later, complaining about the traffic. She really looked pregnant this time. Her belly was out as far as her bust. After signing in, she sat beside me and characteristically started leafing through a magazine. Her lack of social ease was discomforting. I got a whiff of stale cigarette smoke. She was still smoking.

When I asked her about the photograph of the birthfather, she said, "I forgot." I was stunned. We had had two lengthy conversations about it—the last as recently as the night before. Again, she said the reason she had not brought them was out of fear that we wouldn't approve of him. After I reassured her we didn't care how he looked, she said again she would mail a photo with the bills she was accumulating. God, she could be so vexatious.

Claire went into the exam room alone. After a short while, Shelly called us in, saying he didn't have much time because a patient of his was in Labor and Delivery screaming for her epidural. He had to go as soon as possible. He told us that the pregnancy was going fine and that Claire had gained a total of three pounds. He told us she complained of pain in the lower right quadrant of her uterus so he was sending her for another sonogram to make sure everything was all right with the placenta and the baby. I asked when we could determine the gender, and Shelly said Claire would have to ask the sonographer. Claire said mischievously, "Oh, now I can know something that you won't know!"

I asked Shelly to address Claire's smoking. She said she was smoking about a pack every three days. I assumed that was an understatement. He said that a decrease in birth weight was proportionate to the numbers of cigarettes smoked and that decreased birth weight was directly related to increased complications of childbirth. He told her quietly and jokingly to "get her act together." We all realized that only Claire could stop herself and any pressure from her three doctors would likely be met with resistance.

Shelly told us privately that he never received the information from the hospital about the alpha fetoprotein exam—he would call them to follow up. Also, he never received information about the alleged twin pregnancy from the hospital in Ohio. So far, half-way through the pregnancy, we had no confirmation of her twin birth.

After the appointment we went for pizza at the local mall. Claire agreed to tell us the story of the twins and allowed me to take her picture. Her story raised many questions, but we did not challenge her. Both Sam and I had the impression that she made up answers to our requests for clarification on the spur of the moment. Despite this, she reiterated, "This baby I'm carrying is **your** baby and there's no way I'm going home with it after it's born." The only thing she seemed concerned about was how she was going to get home from the hospital. I said that was up to her—it could be one of us, her best friend, or one of our friends, whomever she preferred.

Although we hugged after dinner as we saw her off, we both felt uneasy and dissatisfied with her peculiar brand of openness. I told myself to stop asking questions so that I would stop feeling so bad when I didn't believe the answers. I had to constantly remind myself to just be supportive of Claire and accept what she had to give rather than expecting more. Sometimes, I forget my psychological skills in which support and acceptance are most important. All that really mattered to me was whether Claire and the birthfather would relinquish their parental rights.

It was May twenty-seventh. Claire called. She seemed to be in a good mood. She said her sonogram was scheduled for two o'clock the next afternoon. We were making love when she called—it was the only day of the week when we both were off in the afternoon. Sam would have had me put the machine on, but I wanted to speak with Claire because she had been on my mind all day. More than ever, I didn't think that she really had twins. After our last appointment, I had called all the hospitals in the town where she was living at the time, but none of the medical records departments had heard of her except for the one where her youngest child was born—and they only had records of that child's birth. I was afraid to confront her and yet I couldn't stand the thought that she might be lying to us. If she lied to us about her previous surrogacy, she was capable of anything—even reneging.

In our conversation she talked about how certain she was of giving us this baby—and how she was jealous and envious that we had the love to give it while she did not. She was simply "tapped out" of love in providing for her existing children. She said that she believed that love was important in the baby's life—that it needed two people who loved each other and that she didn't have that. She also said she thought about writing the letter I had requested. I had hoped she would write a letter to Simon so that he would have something of value from his birthmother when he was old enough to appreciate it. If she wanted the baby to know anything when it grew up, it would be that it was loved by her and that she chose us because she thought we could give it what she could not. Because it was unplanned, she said it was even more special. Placing it with us was her way of showing extra care for the child's future. Paradoxically, Claire's way of demonstrating her love for this baby was to give him away—to people who could love him more.

Try as I might, I couldn't get rid of this nagging, soul-wrenching fear that Claire was acting out her own psychological drama and would disappoint us in the end. I diagnosed myself with "burnt child syndrome," a psychological affliction characterized by a fear of closer relationships which affects people who have been emotionally hurt in the past. These "burnt children" tend to avoid taking risks in interpersonal relationships, fearing they'll be hurt again. Having been hurt by Amy, Jennifer, Sandy, Annie and others, I had difficulty trusting any birthmother. Psychologically, I expected that Claire would abandon me, just as Amy had—in the labor and delivery suite at the hospital an hour before the birth. The only thing I wasn't doing was withdrawing. I knew that if we didn't take this risk, we would never have a baby. We got through the pain before. If it happened again, with each others' support, we would get through it again. I was determined not to let anything or anyone stand in my way of creating a family for Sam and me. And I was willing to take any risk.

Claire was excited when she called after her sonogram the next day. The doctor had said the baby weighed two pounds now and from the angles of his sonogram, it appeared to be a boy. She said he seemed quite certain and even pointed out the genitals. He gave her two photos, which she said she'd mail to us. I could hardly fathom the meaning of this news. It was a dream come true. A boy. A son! If only my parents could be here to share in this blessed event. Claire's call dissolved whatever distrust was left, at least for the moment.

Claire reminded me that next week we would have known each other five months. The time was simultaneously speeding and dragging. We only had four months to go before our son would be born. Saying that, I realized that it was going to take me time to get comfortable with using the term, "son," an adaptation I looked forward to with deep satisfaction.

I asked Sam if he wanted to know the sex of the baby, but he said, "No." How could I keep this a secret for four months? He could be so patient, Mr. Natural. Well, I'd do my damnedest to try. And wouldn't you know it—I talked to my mother-in-law later in the week about the sonogram and, without having talked to Sam, she also said, "No. I'd rather wait and be surprised." I chuckled at how those two were so much alike.

Two weeks passed until Claire's next call. It was the second week of June. She seemed quite pleased that I had missed talking with her. Claire was upbeat from her counseling session the previous night. She said she was in counseling more for personal growth than for the pregnancy. She was angry at the birthfather for abandoning her, even though she denied being in love with him. It was a relationship of convenience for both of them. How would that affect her intention to give up his baby? Would it be harder to let go of that reminder of him? Maybe she wouldn't want such a reminder. I amazed myself. I seemed to analyze almost every interaction with Claire in terms of one question only: will she give up the baby? Sometimes I felt like slapping myself.

She said she shared her fears with her therapist and wrote them down in a list. The common denominator was that they all related to abandonment. She was terrified of abandonment and had great difficulty trusting others. She said she still feared that we would abandon her even though she knew others would take the baby if we didn't. I believed our relationship was important to Claire and I felt the same.

Her disclosure prompted me to open up more to her. I shared with Claire my great fear of her abandoning us. As if to reassure me, she said that she went through her closets recently and threw out all the baby things she had from her kids—walker, bassinet, crib, playpen, clothes, blankets, etc. Even so, I felt manipulated again, as if her statement was designed to reassure me. Sam and I both thought that Claire could have a mean streak and we prayed she didn't find any reason to direct it toward us. It was ironic that Claire and I had difficulty trusting each other, yet we were increasingly bound together on this journey which required reciprocal trust.

Claire also told me that she went to the circus not long ago with a friend who had just had a baby. She had enjoyed holding the newborn that afternoon—temporarily. After she gave it back, she felt very tired. That experience confirmed her lack of desire to have another baby. Again, my doubts surfaced. Were her remarks genuine or just designed to create the impression she really didn't want a baby? Her comments, as they so often did, filled me with reassurance and fear. Would I ever get over my insecurity?

By the third week in June it was the twenty-fifth week of the pregnancy. At our fifth appointment with Dr. Shelly, Claire was being examined when we arrived ten minutes early. She had been an hour early. We did not get to see any of the exam, hear the baby's heartbeat or see it on the sonogram, but were invited back to talk with Shelly after the appointment. Upon seeing us in the waiting room, Claire, who looked pretty in a white skirt and red polka dot top, told us, "Shelly moved up my due date by two weeks!" This was an example of Claire's brand of wish-fulfilling thinking. When I asked Shelly about this "change" in the due date, he said that it hadn't changed at all. We could still expect the baby to be born within three days of September thirtieth. Apparently, her fundus had grown substantially. Shelly thought this was going to be a big baby; he predicted approximately nine pounds. Despite the size of the baby, Claire gained a meager two pounds that month. Shelly was unconcerned and said that some, particularly large women, shift their weight when pregnant. Shelly also said that the last sonogram report was excellent and all systems, including the placenta, were working fine. It was reassuring news for worrywart me.

The visit was a quick one, with Shelly prescribing a gestational diabetes test in two weeks. Claire balked at that, saying she didn't need it and hated the taste of the liquid she had to drink to accomplish the test. However, we succeeded in convincing her of the necessity of the test and secured her promise to participate.

Unfortunately, there was no opportunity to talk with Shelly about how to deal with the question of the lack of records of the twin birth and my nagging suspicion that she had made it up. Sam wanted to let it go. For me, it was a constant source of worry. I still privately questioned the veracity of some of Claire's statements. How could I trust her if we could not be sure her claim that she was a surrogate mother before was true? Like a true obsessive, I was stuck on this issue and could not let it go until I was satisfied with the answer.

After the appointment, we took Claire out to dinner at Baltimore's Inner Harbor to help us celebrate our fourteenth anniversary. Sam gave me an "Aloha" shirt and slacks. I had bought us round-trip tickets to Turkey for two weeks in midsummer—the vacation of a lifetime. Everyone said that if we were ever going to take a fabulous vacation, it should be before we have children. Our reservations were confirmed to leave in early August. I wanted to allow plenty of time before the due date so we would not risk missing the birth—even if it was premature.

Claire was friendly and talkative. In the middle of the meal, as if it was an anniversary present, she pulled out a picture of the baby's birthfather. Finally! We expressed our gratitude as we examined the picture. It was a portrait-type photo showing a tall, thin, plain-looking man standing in a dark suit with his attractive, blond wife dressed in a pretty party dress. Wearing horn-rimmed glasses, his red hair long, he had an intellectual look. I couldn't tell that he had green eyes. Claire described him as a "computer nerd: introverted and smart." Her thoughtfulness in bringing his picture further strengthened our growing confidence in her. She took the picture back after we finished looking at it.

Claire also gave us the two sonogram pictures from her last sonogram. Both were very difficult to read for the untrained eye, although the head was clearly visible in one. Her explanation of the one that was supposed to have shown the sex of the baby seemed to make sense. What appeared to be the external genitals were plainly in sight between the upturned legs. I was so heartened that she gave us these pictures. Each act of consideration bolstered my confidence further. We were really on our way to becoming fathers.

She said she was continuing to have a hard time writing the baby the goodbye letter we requested. She had named the baby, as one of the books we had given her had suggested, and she asked us what names we had picked. We told her that we picked Simon if it was a boy and Gloria if it was a girl.

Gloria was an easier name to pick. That was my mother's name. My mother had died suddenly of a stroke seven years earlier. She had always wished for grandchildren from me. Now that we were on the verge of fulfilling her dream as well as our own, I felt sad that she did not live long enough to enjoy a grandchild from me. Yet, how proud I also felt of the legacy she left behind: a book for the families of gay people, *Are You Still My Mother?*, (Warner Books, 1985).

That night, I woke up at three a.m. feeling troubled. I couldn't get back to sleep. I was worrying about Claire's intentions, about the story of the twins, about her honesty, about her conscience, and about her tendency to omit or change details to suit her assessment of the listener's needs. God, would this pregnancy ever end? It had been five months since we had met Claire. Just as I knew nothing would make this baby come sooner, I also knew that nothing would guarantee that it would be ours. All we could do was to be as good to Claire as possible, never forget that she was going to be the mother of our baby, and wait.

Chapter
Twenty-Three

C laire called. Her youngest had chicken pox. I experienced a moment of terror—couldn't that cause blindness or other birth defects in unborn children? Claire was confident that she had already had them, which meant she and the baby were immune. We called Shelly, who confirmed that there was no danger to the baby as long as Claire had already had the disease. Even if she hadn't, however, the baby would be at most risk if it occurred in the first trimester or in the last ten days. At this point, towards the end of the second trimester, the baby was as protected as it could be. Please, God, let no virus hurt this defenseless baby.

In the next week, Claire called twice more. We had good, heart-to-heart talks about the impending birth. She was now in weekly counseling and seemed to be benefiting. It seemed to help her to open up to me. She talked about trust and how hard it was for her to rely on anyone but herself. She hated becoming dependent on others. She feared that we might fall through and leave her in the lurch. She knew we were reliable, which was why she chose us, but her fear of abandonment operated on an emotional level, just as mine did. She raised the concern that the adoption agency might not give us the baby right away. She wanted to be sure that we would be able to take the baby home from the hospital directly. She didn't want it to go to foster care while the legal papers were being processed.

Because we were interacting so well, and because we had begun to trust each other more, I finally expressed my lingering concern about her lack of a birth record for her twins. She was at a loss for words and said she would try to dig them up to reassure me. She denied that they were born anywhere else. I wondered if she was caught in a lie but could offer no different story or if there was another explanation, such as a legal expungement of the records. The doubt would not let me rest in peace—and I was never to get those records.

On Independence Day weekend, Claire visited our home for the second time, this time with all of her children. Claire had the day off and decided to take an excursion. The weather was gloomy, however, and we were only able to swim for an hour before it started to rain. Claire wouldn't tell the kids how she knew us, nor had she told them that we would be adopting their baby brother or sister. Happily, we had a good time. It was fun to get acquainted with her children—like having a sneak preview. I imagined our baby might be like one of them.

I was a bit unclear about her agenda for the day. Did she want to give us a chance to see what kind of children she made? Did she want to test us, using her children to see what kind of parents we would make? Did she just want to get closer? Or should we just take her at face value and accept that all she really wanted was to offer her kids a fun day trip with some nice, new friends? During her visit, I showed her the video of the ninetieth birthday party we hosted for Grandma Fay the year before. The tape demonstrated our great relationships with our families and I was sure she was impressed. I also showed her our home study report from the adoption agency, something that every prospective adoptive parent has to have. We read the nine-page document together. It was an extensive report on our life history and answered all of Claire's questions about our past. This was the document the judge would have to find satisfactory in order to grant our petition to adopt.

Hopefully, reading the home study allayed whatever lingering fears of abandonment Claire might still have had. For the rest of the day, we played hide and seek, took pictures and had lots of fun. I think we made quite an impression. Another good sign appeared that day. Claire gave us the birthfather's picture. Previously, she had only shown it to us. Now, it was ours. Someday, it would be Simon's or Gloria's. When they left, Claire's youngest held my hand tight as they were leaving. "I don't want to leave, I'm attached to you. But I'm attached to you," she kept saying. As they left, I felt pleased, thinking we had passed the "kid" test, if there was one.

Two weeks later, I was working at my computer in what would soon be Simon's room. To my left was a window framing our front yard. In the background on a slope facing the window were azaleas, rhododendrons, a dogwood tree and ground cover of hypericum, pachysandra and hostas. The yard never looked so glorious. Just outside the window, not six feet away, were a mother robin and four newly-hatched chicks perched in their nest in a branch of the torulosa juniper. For weeks, I had been seeing a bird fly out of this tree each time I passed it, but it wasn't until recently that I actually saw the nest and its eggs. Now, the expectant mother had hatched her brood and was keeping it warm and fed inches from this special room. I took this as a good omen—one which heralded our impending fatherhood.

That was the week of our sixth appointment—Week Twenty-nine. Claire had officially entered the third trimester and the baby would have a good chance of surviving if it were born now. Claire was a half hour late, due to traffic. Shelly's office was without power because of a summer storm which had blown through an hour earlier. Shelly was sitting out in the darkened waiting room with Sam when I came in. They were talking about Shelly's new home and his family's impending move. We didn't talk about the baby or the adoption and all of us were relaxed. Sam and I looked forward to more frequent visits with our friend and his family as they would soon be practically neighbors.

Claire finally arrived, looking pretty and fit in her new, short summer hairdo. She was in and out in five minutes. The appointments continued to amaze me in their brevity. I was always impressed by how little there was to do other than monitor the baby's growth until it was born. Claire gained three more pounds, which pleased Shelly, and her gestational diabetes test results were normal. She was as healthy as she had predicted. Her belly continued to surprise me in its increasing girth. I hugged her when she came in. A genuine bond had finally developed between us.

After the appointment we went to a nearby restaurant and ordered barbecued rib platters. We ate and talked for two hours at a corner table. Claire described in more detail what it was like feeling this child inside. She said she could feel its bottom on her right side and its head on her lower left side. She noticed it was shifting position and its head was now in a four o'clock position. She joked that when it got to the six o'clock position, she'd be ready to deliver. Since her naval was still "in" she wasn't quite ready to give birth. She compared herself to a turkey with a pop-up plastic timer which indicated when the bird was cooked enough. When her belly-button popped out, the baby would be ready! We had a good laugh and our meeting was the most relaxed and enjoyable we'd had so far. She spoke in terms of "your baby" this and "your baby" that. My fear and doubts were fading. This was really going to happen—and soon.

We also talked about our birth plan—how we wanted things to be in the hospital. Claire did not want the baby placed on her stomach. She wanted to go to her room to sleep after the baby and afterbirth were delivered. We agreed that I would be the first one to hold the baby after it was born and Sam would cut the cord. I would be able to hold, feed and bathe it in the nursery. When Claire was ready to see the baby the next day, she would ask the nurse to bring it. We agreed to videotape and photograph the entire labor and delivery.

The excitement I felt was slow and deep. I was increasingly filled with disbelief, wonderment, and even pain. Whenever I thought of parenting, I thought of my mother. How happy she would be that I was having a baby. How wonderful she was to me as a mother. How much she taught me to love and how I could pass on her love now, finally, to my child. My eyes filled at one point during our meal as I saw Sam feeling Claire's belly.

I was also terrified. Frightened of what I was getting myself into. Frightened of not measuring up to the job. Frightened of being too old, too impatient, too set in my ways. Frightened of being overwhelmed by the needs and demands of an infant. Frightened of losing my work, my hobbies, my friends, my independence.

Despite this, I knew in my soul that this was the direction my life, our life, would take. Our future lay with our family of three. And who knew, maybe four! I found comfort in writing to our unborn son.

Dear Simon,

It's been a long time since I've written you. Part of the reason for this is that I've been so caught up with your coming that I haven't stopped to think of you as a person—just your arrival. I've also been struggling with disbelief that you really are coming and that soon you'll be home. My trust for your birthmother has grown considerably over the months we've known her, although it's been hard for me to trust her completely. But our last couple of visits have been fun, both the social visit with your half-siblings and last night's visit with the OB. You'll be here soon and we're starting to prepare. We'll move my desk into the solarium, get you a bassinet, a layette and other things to get you started in your new room.

Also, I'm going to have to learn how to feed you and bathe you and change your diapers (hourly, I'm told), hold and rock you, and enable you to feel secure and loved and okay. Did you know I've never changed a diaper before? Don't worry, though. I may be a man and not have learned all this mothering stuff, but I'm smart and ambitious and can do anything I set my mind to. I'll take care of you completely (with Daddy Sam's help, of course). I promise. See you soon, son.

Your loving father, Dad Ken

July twentieth, I called the adoption agency to arrange the consultation for our adoption. We scheduled it for one p.m. in the agency's office. From there we would pre-register at the hospital and then have our appointment at Dr. Shelly's, all on August twenty-sixth, about one month prior to the birth. It was nerve-wracking to have made this call because I hated relinquishing control and that was what would happen once we were in the hospital and in the court system. I trusted that the agency could handle the placement and the relinquishment, but hospitals were public places. I feared encountering busybody nurses, do-good social workers, and risk managers who just wanted to limit their hospital's liability exposure. I was so afraid of our losing control that I'd even contemplated not going to a hospital, but rather having Simon born in a birthing center. The social worker at the adoption agency said that I had to keep a "low profile" in the hospital because nurses and social workers don't generally like adoptions and some would do what they could to frustrate plans. I told the lawyer at the agency that the birthmother and I had a birthing plan which included my being in the delivery room. The lawyer said this was possible if I pretended that I was the father. His remark irritated me because I would be the father—I didn't have to pretend anything. With each approaching day, I found it harder and harder to contain my emotions.

Chapter
Twenty-Four

*I*t was now mid-August and almost a month had passed since our last obstetrician's appointment. Much had happened in that time. Sam and I took our two-week trip to Turkey. What an odyssey. This was to be the last independent vacation we would take for some time, our last "great adventure" as a couple. We traveled throughout the country, seeing ancient ruins, meeting people from all over the globe, and glorying in the ten thousand year old civilization of the ancient Hittites, Romans, Greeks, Christians, Byzantines, Ottoturks and Turks.

Not a day went by, however, that I didn't think of Simon's approach. Despite the fact that his arrival was less than a month away, he was still an abstraction. The reality of his impending birth had still not sunk in. We returned to the States exhausted, having travelled non-stop for twenty-four hours. David picked us up at the airport—good friend that he is. We had dinner with David and Tom later that night, but it was a short visit.

I called Claire twice that evening, as I had promised before I left. Each time there was no answer until about ten thirty, when she called me with the news. She had gone into labor the previous Tuesday and had had to go to the Emergency Room. The E.R. called

Shelly, who gave instructions for them to administer a drug to stop the contractions. She was at thirty-two weeks and the baby still had two months to go to full term, or at the very least, one month until it could be safely delivered. I was dismayed not to have been there. According to Shelly, Claire had an "irritable uterus." Women with such conditions frequently had premature contractions. It was almost as if every cell of Claire's wanted the baby out of her body. Shelly put her on bed rest for the remainder of the pregnancy, although Sam and I feared that she would not comply. Shelly made clear to Claire the risk to the baby should it be born prematurely. Claire agreed to do her best to try to keep still and keep the baby inside at least until the end of the month. She did say, however, that we'd better go out and start shopping, because we were going to be fathers sooner than we thought. I prayed that this child would not be born prematurely and that we wouldn't have to spend our first days as parents visiting a neonatal intensive care unit.

Shelly's order of bed rest worried me for Claire's sake. Unable to work, her income would drop, even though she had disability insurance through her job. On bed rest, she wouldn't be able to care for her children as normal and I feared the family would be put under additional stress. I wished we could help her through this period—with a housekeeper or nanny or just money for groceries, but our lawyer told us that the courts forbid financial assistance by adoptive parents. Marla had told us of one case in which the judge fined the parents and made the birthmother repay them for maternity clothing they had purchased for her. Thankfully, we were in the home stretch.

The impending arrival led to a flurry of activity. I called the adoption agency to move up our appointment to two days hence. At least we wouldn't be caught off guard at the hospital. Claire was feeling contractions every thirty minutes and was starting to feel more than her normal physical discomfort. I prayed she could hold on and not do anything which would precipitate a premature birth. Shelly said that even though she had gained only a total of three pounds from the outset of the pregnancy so far, her fundal height was good and the baby was a healthy size. The excitement was a slow burn.

The day after I arrived home from Turkey, I had a full day

scheduled with patients. Then, I spent the following three days at the American Psychological Association annual convention in Washington. As an active member of the Association's Division Forty-Four, the Society for the Psychological Study of Lesbian and Gay Issues, I volunteered to serve on a task force of gay and lesbian families. I hoped I wouldn't be over-committed.

Sam went to Sears and bought some articles for our layette. He also looked at cribs. He bought diapers, receiving blankets, a hooded bath towel, snap shirts, "onesies," washcloths, bottles, nipples, safety pins and bottle liners. Looking at these tiny articles of clothing spread out in front of me as I assigned them to various drawers brought back that feeling of unreality. Were we really going to have a baby? We're too old. We're gay. We don't even have a room for him yet. But even as I thought the words, I knew the doubts were evaporating. Simon was coming home at last. Hurry up and get ready!

Two days after we returned from Turkey, on August eighteenth, Claire and I met with the attorney at the adoption agency. By this time, Sam, Claire and I had agreed that we would go the single-parent adoption route and petition the court at a future date for a second-parent adoption for the co-parent. I made a list of things to bring to the meeting—questions about how the process would go, Claire's divorce decree, and our birth plan. I called Claire at nine a.m. as planned and went over the birth plan with her. She said it sounded fine to her. She told me that she couldn't find her divorce decree and that she had to stop at her lawyer's to pick up a copy. As the agency was a two hour drive from each of our homes, the trip gave us time to contemplate the enormity of what we were about to do.

I got there fifteen minutes early. The building was not what I had expected. I thought it would be a bigger, fancier place. It was a two-person office on the second floor of a slightly run-down building in a plain, residential/commercial neighborhood one block off the main road of a small, middle class Washington suburb. The lawyer and his assistant were the only two people in the suite.

A half hour passed and Claire hadn't arrived. I went in by myself and hoped Claire would call if she were lost. She did. She had become frantic when she couldn't find the building. I calmed her down and arranged to stand outside at the corner as a landmark until she saw me. She was only five minutes from the agency. After turning into the parking lot, she parked her car and sighed in relief. She remarked that even though I looked strange with the beard I had grown while in Turkey, she was glad to see me. As we mounted the steep, narrow staircase, I found myself wondering how an adoption agency could be on the second floor of a building without an elevator. The steep, narrow stairs would challenge any pregnant woman.

The lawyer was friendly and thorough in his explanation of the ways in which the adoption could take place. He explained the agency's role and informed us it was Claire's responsibility to let the hospital know that she would be giving up the baby for adoption. He said the agency would send a notary seventy-two hours after the birth to obtain her and the birthfather's relinquishment signatures. The lawyer also asked for negative HIV test results from both of us. The only thing Claire wanted to be sure of was that no one else but Sam and I would get the baby. Over lunch afterwards, I told Claire that I missed not being able to talk with the baby throughout the pregnancy. She said that since she was on bed-rest now, she would accommodate me if I wanted to talk to the baby. Our next meeting would be at the doctor's office in two weeks, then every week thereafter until the birth.

Claire called three days later. Her contractions were now twenty minutes apart. She felt the birth getting close, despite the fact that she had six weeks left to go. We were to have company that weekend. Three of my cousins, their wives and children, my uncle, his wife and two kids. I was really looking forward to this visit and anticipated a smaller scale family reunion than the ninetieth birthday party for Grandma the year before at the same time. Wouldn't that be something if I became a father with so many members of my family around?

A couple of days later, Claire called again. She woke up at two a.m. with contractions and felt that she had better go to the doctor in the morning as she believed she was experiencing "first show." This was the loosening of the mucus plug with slight bleeding, the precursor of labor. She would be driven to the hospital by a friend and I would meet her there at noon. I was getting more excited as each hour passed. Incredibly, we were not ready. We had neither a crib, cradle nor even a car seat. The adoption agency lawyer had not mailed me our agreement and we didn't have a pediatrician lined up. We hadn't even moved the furniture to accommodate a crib. We'd been avoiding doing all this work for fear something might go wrong. Now we could delay no more. Our work for the week was cut out for Sam and me. Make way for Simon!

The next morning Sam and I went shopping for more baby items. Instead of being scary (what would we do with all these baby things if we didn't get the baby?), it was fun shopping together. This was something we didn't normally do. As we walked down the aisles, I became fascinated with the tiny clothes on the racks. It was like shopping for a doll! But how could we choose things? I never played with dolls in my life. A part of me felt like I didn't belong in this section of the store. My old sexist tapes were playing: shopping for infants was a woman's work. But there were no women in this family, just two Dads. God, I wished our mothers were with us. Each article of clothing—the tiny socks and booties, the nightgowns with drawstrings at the bottoms, the hooded receiving blankets—was new and strange. What did we need now? How many would we need of each? As mundane as I normally found shopping, this trip was memorable for the sheer excitement of the anticipation both Sam and I felt. We left the store with bags and bags of goodies.

After shopping, Sam went to keep his appointments with his patients in the office and I went to the hospital to meet Claire. When I arrived at noon, she had already been there a half hour and was in the examining room hooked up to fetal heart and uterine contraction monitors. The baby's heart, amplified by the machine, sounded strong and steady. I was proud and excited to hear it. The tape showed that she was having contractions every twenty minutes. The nurse did not report bloody show, but the pelvic exam revealed she was dilated two centimeters. After consulting with Shelly, the nurse told us that Claire was not in labor and that she should go home and return when the contractions were ten minutes apart.

Claire was disappointed. She really wanted to get this over with. I wondered how well she was adhering to the bed rest advice. I told her what the doctor had told me: that she could go at least another month like this and might well not have the baby for as many as six more weeks. Shelly said that if Claire went into labor in the next ten days that they would do their best to stop it. She was not a happy camper. We had arranged for Claire to spend the last two weeks or so of the pregnancy with us—just to be closer to the hospital. That could be as much as a month away.

The room in the house we had chosen for Simon's nursery was actually a den which had been a part of our master bedroom. We had it walled off in anticipation of Simon's arrival so that it was now a separate, if small room. It was perfect for a nursery—adjacent to our bedroom, small, yet with three large windows. We chose pastel-colored wallpaper with a clouds and rainbow motif and had fun hanging mobiles, a wall sculpture and new pictures on the walls. I imagined that our experience and excitement in building and decorating this room was a collective one shared by most couples who prepared a nursery in expectation of their first child.

By Labor Day, Claire had entered the thirty-sixth week of her pregnancy. The weeks since her premature labor passed uneventfully. Claire had her individual appointment with the adoption agency social worker, which went well. That was a relief because it lent further credence to Claire's intentions. She steadfastly reiterated to the counselor her intention to give the baby up to us for adoption. My doubts now were just passing shadows with none of the potency of my fears early in the pregnancy.

We also had another appointment with the obstetrician. Dr. Shelly said Claire was still dilated two centimeters. At this point, Claire wanted labor to be induced, complaining that she had fulfilled Shelly's requirements by going the rest of the month. Shelly advised us that he could not induce labor until Claire was at least four centimeters dilated. Further, he cautioned her to make every effort to keep the baby in her for at least one more week. Claire took that as permission to dance the polka in eight days. Her entire focus seemed to be to have the baby out of her body. She wanted her life back to normal—to return to her job, her family and her routines.

After the doctor's appointment we went to the hospital to take a guided tour of the labor and delivery areas. Sam, Claire and I were the only ones on the tour, enabling us to comfortably ask questions about if and how babies being given up for adoption were handled differently at this hospital. The nurse who led us around was also pregnant and due the day before Claire. On our tour, we rehearsed the scenario we would undergo when our time came. We learned where we could park close to the hospital entrance and how to check in quickly. From there, we would go to the monitoring room where the decision would be made whether or not to admit Claire.

If the doctor said so, Claire would be admitted to the birthing room, which was the next stop on our tour. This is where the main event would take place. The room was large and had a birthing bed, television, private bath, bassinet with an overhead heater (the "warming table") and curtained windows. The birthing room had its own separate waiting room with a sink and refrigerator in it for family members to wait close by. Claire would be in labor and have the baby in that same room unless a C-section had to be done, in which case she would be taken to the operating room, which was next on our tour. We peeked into one of the three operating rooms and learned that if she needed surgery, only one of us would be allowed to be present with her. If she had to have a general anesthetic, no one would be able to be with her in the operating room except the surgical team.

Next stop was the obstetrical floor and the nursery, where there were private and semi-private rooms. We observed that most new mothers in the hospital at the time of our tour were rooming-in with their babies. In fact, the nursery was empty. It was there, however, that we would feed, bathe, rock and hold Simon until we took him home from the hospital. The nursery, then, was going to be our not-so-private room. It didn't faze me in the least that our displays of affection to the baby and between ourselves would be public but it crossed my mind that some of the nurses might be surprised to see two male parents attending to the baby.

As we walked through the operating room area, terrifically sad memories flooded back. This was the same hospital in which we lost Amy's baby. It took all my energy to keep from breaking down in the corridor. Suddenly, it seemed like yesterday that I was comforting Amy before she delivered her baby. It was actually twenty months ago. I had a flashback of being ushered from the labor suite by her social worker and never seeing her or the baby again. It was so painful; it was momentarily hard to realize that this was a different situation, a different woman, a different baby, a more certain outcome.

My fear and nervousness would soon be over as we began our new life as a family. We were just about ready to receive our son or daughter. A friend pointed out to me recently that by building a shed, planting a perennial garden and creating a baby's room, I was nesting just like most other expectant parents. I had bought one of almost every item I had seen in a baby catalog and the nursery was almost ready. But before Simon came, I needed to finish the shed that I'd been building all summer. I called it my garden folly because it was so much more elaborate in its contemporary architectural design than the term "shed" implied. All the lumber was assembled and I had already done most of the work. The next weekend we were to have a barn-raising. Ten of our friends would help us to erect the two by four wall frames I had pre-assembled and to sheath the skeleton in plywood. I would leave it to sub-contractors to install the heavy cantilevered roof trusses and apply the stucco skin and blue-green metal standing-seam roof.

As we rounded the corner into Week Thirty-seven, we had our barn-raising. It was funny hearing all that hammering and nailing from a gaggle of middle-aged gay guys. Half the group were doctors, most of whom wielded their hammers with the enthusiasm and dexterity of a toddler flailing a stick. Ironically, the best workers were two straight friends—a couple who came over with their four-month old baby. They hammered furiously while their baby slept in his stroller. I was amazed that he could tolerate all that noise and was heartened to see that having an infant didn't have to mean giving up the outdoor hobbies which I loved. We erected the four walls and sheathed one of them with plywood that day. Afterwards, we had a cook-out. Although it had been cloudy all day, it did not rain and it was warm enough to soak in the hot-tub. At the end of the day I felt proud and happy to have built this structure, appreciative of our friends for helping, and tickled that I had probably provided them with the only barn they would ever help raise in their lives.

Chapter
Twenty-Five

C laire's thirtieth birthday arrived. The next day she would come to stay with us until she gave birth. It would be interesting having her with us for this extended period of time. I had genuinely grown fond of her, although some of her idiosyncrasies still drove me to distraction. All of us would feel safer having her at our home. We didn't want to risk her going into labor over one hundred miles away and not being able to get her to our hospital in time.

I called Claire and sang "Happy Birthday" over the telephone. She was pleased to hear from me and told me about the fun she had and the presents she had received at the birthday party her family threw for her. She was preparing to make the trip to our house. I sensed that Claire, too, was becoming concerned about unexpectedly having the baby up there. Should we get a waterproof sheet for her bed in case her water broke in her sleep? I didn't want to embarrass her. What would Emily Post say?

My friend David called. He revealed that Sam's assistant and the nurses from the hospital were planning a surprise baby shower for us the next Thursday. This would be in addition to the one David was going to host for our friends. I was touched. How many expectant couples have two baby showers? I would refer to these events in the future as our Gayby Showers.

Our obstetrical appointments were now scheduled every Wednesday. The next one was in the afternoon of Week Thirty-eight, the day Claire would arrive to stay. Sam and I arrived at Shelly's office on time, only to be greeted by Claire in the parking lot. She had already been seen; the appointment was over. She handed me my appointment card for next week and said, "Well, I'm still dilated two centimeters but I'm fifty-seven per cent effaced! What does that mean?" I was so disappointed to have missed her meeting and missed an opportunity to meet with the doctor that I asked if we could go back in and speak with Shelly briefly. We saw that the waiting room was filled. It appeared busier than I'd ever seen. Shelly was with a patient but came up to the desk shortly and said that Claire was doing perfectly and that she was free to have the baby any time she wanted. If she went into labor now, he would deliver the baby. She had gone the term, the baby was healthy, the mother was healthy, and all was ready. I asked if he could estimate how long it would be until the baby came. "Not," he chirped with a mischievous smile.

From the doctor's office, we decided to go right home and help Claire settle in. We were so relieved when we had her safely ensconced in our home. We had dreaded the thought of her going into labor in Pennsylvania and having to go to her local hospital, where, upon our arrival, we would have to explain ourselves to the hospital staff. They wouldn't be prepared for our unusual situation. Now when she went into labor, within twenty minutes we could be at our hospital, which was prepared.

Claire was relieved to be with us. She said that she had been experiencing pressure at home and needed to get away. When we arrived home from our appointment, as we were making dinner, I asked her about that pressure. She said that her parents were repeatedly asking her if she really knew what she was doing, if she was at peace with her decision. Claire had to reassure them to make them feel better. That did not sit right with her because she was the one who needed reassurance. She had to focus her attention on having this baby and preparing for the separation, not on comforting her well-meaning but emotionally draining family. I was impressed with her insight.

Still, I was frightened. My greatest fear, that old bugaboo, was that she was using us, as Amy used us, for protection until the baby was born. And then she'd say "sayonara." She observed that I wasn't trusting of people. I was again impressed with her insight. Now, more than ever, I was convinced that the problem wasn't Claire's trustworthiness, but my distrustfulness.

Later that night Claire gave me a sloppily folded piece of paper. It was the birth-father's signed and notarized intent to relinquish his parental rights. Hallelujah! Another step completed. It was a relief to get the first written indication that the baby's birthfather didn't want this child. This scrap of paper, regardless of its unenforceability, removed whatever lingering doubt I harbored about the baby's adoptability.

However anxious Claire was to have the baby and return home, I knew that she was having a marvelous time with us. We hot-tubbed each day of the weekend, late into the night and she quickly got used to being waited on and pampered at "Morgen-Westrick Acres" as if it were a spa vacation. On Friday night we did her favorite activity—"malling." We went to our local shopping mall where a fancy new department store had just opened. We all enjoyed that, and going for pizza afterwards. From there, we bought ice cream and went to Dave and Tom's, where we introduced her to our friends, ate the ice cream and chatted. I think by introducing Claire to Simon's uncles-to-be and our friends to our birthmother, the impending birth became that much more real for all of us.

Saturday, Sam finished wallpapering the baby's room and I worked on the shed. Dave, his cousin Rex, and Tom came over and hung around the pool. Then, we had a dinner of hard-shelled crabs and played bridge. Although it was her first time playing, Claire was a quick study. She had good card sense, something which bode well for our baby's potential to be a fourth for bridge. Claire plainly enjoyed the dinner and the new friends she had made. One could see that she was at her best in a crowd. Also present were another gay doctor and his lover, a sociologically educational experience for Claire. Sunday, it was more of the same. The weather was perfect and we worked throughout the day and played into the evening. After dinner, we watched some of the videos of our trip to Turkey. Claire found them fascinating. It was the first time we had watched them since returning home.

Claire disclosed that the day before she had more pain and heavier contractions than normal. She thought she could feel the baby shifting inside her. We assumed it was taking its position in the birth canal. Then, another friend, Sam's doctor, stopped by and dropped off his hand-made mahogany cradle for us to borrow. It was a lovely, simple rocking affair which had symbolic value as well since it represented the support of our straight friends. The next morning, other friends called to express their concern, curiosity and good wishes. Everyone in our circle seemed to be sharing the suspense.

On September fourteenth, Claire accompanied me to pick up the crib I had bought. It's hard to describe the feeling I had when our pregnant birthmother helped load the car and assemble the crib once we got it home. I wondered aloud about whether this was her gift to the baby. It seemed so important for her to assist in readying his bed. It's a lovely memory that I will have forever, the two of us putting together that crib in the nursery.

Claire said she wanted to see the priest of the local church before she went to the hospital about baptizing the baby. I became afraid, thinking that a homonegative priest could ruin the adoption. I called a former patient who had once been a Catholic priest to ask for a recommendation of a priest Claire could see who would not be homonegative. He referred me to Father John, someone with whom I had spoken the year before concerning the gay rights amendment.

Over the telephone, Father John taught me some interesting facts about baptism. Baptism normally was the first of three steps in a person's entering a community of faith in Catholic life. The ceremony requires the parent/s to promise to raise the child Catholic. He told me that if Claire was going to give the baby up for adoption, she would not be able to make such a promise. Further, she knew the baby would not be raised Catholic. I managed to keep my insecurity about whether this would undermine Claire's resolve to go through with the adoption to myself. Hopefully, meeting with Father John would resolve whatever questions Claire had on the subject.

Father John saw Claire the next afternoon while we had our surprise baby shower. Although I knew about it in advance, Sam was quite surprised. About thirty nurses were present, people who had worked with Sam for years. There were balloons, great food, cake and much laughter over opening the presents. One of the guests even made us hats with all the ribbons and bows from the presents, which we were obliged to wear. I wondered where that custom came from. I would have bet no one in that house had ever been to a baby shower for two expectant fathers before.

Claire came back from her visit with a sense of peacefulness, content in her acceptance that the baby would not be baptized. That evening, at her insistence, we viewed our videotape of the baby shower. Claire appeared to enjoy our group's camaraderie, but I couldn't help wondering if she was hurting inside. She showed no evidence of emotional pain over the shower being for her baby but not for her.

Mid-week we visited Shelly's office for our scheduled appointment. Claire and I drove in my car and Sam met us there. All three of us were becoming increasingly anxious as the birth approached. I asked if we could meet with Shelly after his exam of Claire. It wasn't long before Shelly asked us back to his office and sat the three of us down in front of his desk. His heavy brows furrowed, he looked serious and perplexed. It was bad news. We were about to find out why Claire had greater pain than usual over the weekend.

The baby was in a breach position. Shelly described it as bad luck. When he inserted his hand in Claire's vagina to feel the baby's head, it wasn't there! By digital exam, the doctor determined that the baby's head was at Claire's upper right side and its bottom was pointed down. He explained that, although not common, it was not necessarily alarming. He tried to assure us that most breach births appeared so from early in pregnancy. In Claire's case, the head was down, in the vertex position, from the beginning. It was just bad luck that it rotated up. Apparently, babies are most comfortable seated head down in the pelvic saddle. In cases like this, it was more than likely that the baby would find the correct position to prepare for a vaginal birth. In the position at the moment, it was less likely that labor would be soon, because Claire needed the pressure of the baby's head on her cervix to precipitate labor.

The doctor scheduled our next exam in five days instead of the usual seven. Shelly said if the baby was still in the breach position then, we would have to wait longer. If the baby's head was engaged by next week, he would induce labor. He didn't want to chance the baby's becoming disengaged again.

We might have a baby as early as next Monday. For the time being, we could do nothing but wait. Claire confided in me afterwards over lunch that she was afraid that she had disappointed us. I reassured her that we thanked God for her every day and that this was not her fault.

That night we rented a movie starring Michael Douglas and Melanie Griffith—a story of World War II heroes. It had a happy ending, something we all needed. Afterwards, we took a midnight soak in the hot tub. It was to be one of our last. I was now confident that things would work out and that the baby would turn over the weekend.

By Sunday, I finished building what I could of the shed. Now Claire was truly free to have this baby. We had been joking that it couldn't come out until I had finished, like Sheherezade's thousand and one nights. That night we played bridge with David, continuing to be impressed with how well Claire had picked up the game. We had a marvelous dinner of barbecued pork from the grill, hot sauerkraut with fried onions, salad and roasted potatoes. David brought a chocolate ice cream pie and fresh whipped cream. A happy calm before a happier storm.

To pass the time, we'd been making predictions about when and how the baby was going to come. Claire thought it would not have turned by Monday so Shelly would try to manually turn it *in utero* and deliver it on Tuesday. I thought it would have started to turn and he would say let's wait a few more days. I didn't think he would have to do a C-section. Sam thought he'd do nothing but wait until the due date came in ten days. My gut feeling was that Simon would come before week's end.

That night, before dinner, Claire uncharacteristically asked me a serious question: What contact with her did we envision having after the baby was born? Having considered this question from the time we wrote our surrogate mother contract, when we first met, I told her I anticipated sending her pictures and news of the baby at Christmas over the years, and hoped that she would do the same. As the baby grew up, I anticipated we would tell him where he came from gradually, in response to his questions. Simon would have to make his own decision about whether and when he would want to meet his birth-parents. I had long ago accepted that I could not foresee or solve all the problems we might have raising an adopted child.

Claire's question made me consider that, since contemplating a surrogate mother arrangement nine months ago, maybe the rules had changed. Decisions we made about how things would be after the baby came and how we would relate to the birth-mother after the birth, now seemed quite irrelevant. I sensed Claire was feeling sad at that moment—not only over preparing to say goodbye to her baby, but also to us. Or was it my own sadness? At that moment, I realized I was really going to miss her.

Monday brought the fateful doctor's appointment and Week Thirty-nine, just one week before the forty week full term status. Claire was examined by Shelly just after lunch. I was in the waiting room. Sam was seeing his own patients in the office. It didn't take long to find out. Hooray! The baby had turned—it was in the vertex position. It was now ready to be born.

Because of the baby's now having turned twice, once out of position and once back into it, Shelly said that he would induce labor if it didn't come by itself within the next two days. We pulled out our calendars and decided on Thursday, September twenty-fourth, at eight a.m. It amazed me that we could schedule this childbirth as if it were a dental appointment.

Shelly explained the induction procedure. First, he would examine Claire. If the baby was still head-down, he would inject a hormonal gel into her vagina. The gel would stimulate uterine contractions which would, in turn, precipitate true labor. He advised us that a second, third or even fourth dose of the gel might be necessary. If a good, strong labor didn't come by the second dose, he would then administer pitocin, which would surely do the trick. If all went as planned, Simon would come on Thursday afternoon, September twenty-fourth.

I was so happy, I could hardly contain my excitement. I called Sam immediately after the appointment. He had already called Shelly's office. He was ecstatic, too. Everything was happening just the way we had hoped and dreamed. Then David called. We set the date of our post-birth baby shower. I found myself praying silently. Please, God, don't let anything happen to spoil this miracle.

The night before the birth, I came home from work about nine p.m. I found a letter to the baby from Claire lying open on the breakfast table. I was so grateful that she wrote him something, I gave her a hug. Before putting it away, I read it to myself:

Sept. 22

My Dear Child,

Our time together will soon be over. I have treasured the time we have spent alone. Your every kick and movement within me brought great joy and happiness.

When I met Ken and Sam in January the love that radiated from their eyes told me there could be no other place for you to grow. Your parents hold on to the most important keys as parents. They are the keys of love and hope. Love of others and hope for a strong future.

As you grow in a world filled with obstacles, Ken and Sam will be there for you every step of the way. I pray the bond we share now will remain with you throughout your life. I will always carry love in my heart for you.

Love, Your Birthmother
Claire

I sealed the letter and put it in a safe place. This treasure will belong to Simon some day. I was so grateful that she finally wrote it. Those simple words will mean so much to this adopted child.

The next day, Sam and Claire went "malling." Sam said he encouraged her to walk as much as possible, hoping that would precipitate labor. It didn't. However, on Wednesday morning Claire said she'd been vomiting, a sign that she took to mean that she was in early labor.

To me, Wednesday night felt like the night before Christmas. We dined out at our favorite local restaurant, a Greek place, where we drank non-alcoholic champagne. We congratulated ourselves on our success at completing the pregnancy just as we had planned it nine months before when we met as total strangers in Claire's living room. We conspiratorially took turns guessing exactly what time the baby would come, what his weight and the color of his hair would be, or if he would have any hair at all. Claire thought Simon's hair would be red and that he would have plenty because she had heartburn throughout the pregnancy. I just wanted him to come out with two eyes, one nose, ten fingers and ten toes.

We got home from dinner at eleven p.m., satisfied, but not tired. Sam had pre-heated the hot tub for one last soak before the birth. We donned our bathing suits and slid into the warm, still water as soon as we got home. We left the jets off, so it was quiet and peaceful. The warmth of the water became a tonic which soothed us before retiring. Claire had fallen in love with the hot tub and its landscaped setting. She felt light in the spa, comfortable, and safe. The moon was a silver crescent and the dark, clear, night sky permitted us to view the brighter stars and planets. Without speaking, we all shared the same apprehension about what was to come the following morning: the birth of a baby boy Sam and I had already named Simon and the permanent separation of Simon from his mother. I could not contemplate accepting Simon without acknowledging Claire's loss. How does one say goodbye to a baby? Was Claire going to be all right?

After soaking in silence for a long time, I began to speak. I acknowledged our special friendship, the wonderful journey we had been on and the miracle that was to come the following day. Sam and I thanked Claire again and promised to keep the baby safe, love him and nurture him until he was ready to be an independent adult. We promised we would tell him that Claire loved him while he was inside her and that she would never forget him.

As I prepared for bed that night, I reflected on the years of anticipation that had preceded this birth: my earliest thoughts in high school and college, conversations with Sam over our fourteen years together, and the numerous disappointments in our journey to create a family. I thought of the wonderful people we met along the way, people who encouraged us and empowered us to keep trying and never give up—our families and friends. They rooted for us, wished and hoped along with us that this time, Simon would come to us for good. I thought of my deceased parents looking down on Sam and me from heaven, guarding us, protecting us and the baby, feeling as happy as we were that we were having their grandchild. I felt myself welling up with the sadness that they hadn't lived long enough to meet this child.

We went to sleep late that night, each of us pensive, peaceful, excited, and frightened all at once. Would tomorrow be our dream come true or yet another horrible nightmare? Late in the pregnancy, Claire had fallen into the habit of holding her hands under her swollen belly. That was my last image of her that night in the shadow of the stars by the pool in the garden as I drifted off to dreamlessness. Our new life was going to begin in less than twenty-four hours.

Chapter
Twenty-Six

S am and I awoke at six a.m. without the help of the alarm. We were alert, wide-awake and ready to get going. After showers, light breakfasts, and packing the items on our "Hospital Checklist," we were ready to leave by seven fifteen. Claire was up even earlier and had finished her breakfast before we were out of the shower. She was even more anxious to get on with it. No wonder.

Previously, when I imagined how the morning of the birth might be, I thought of the old "Dick Van Dyke Show." The three of us would be bumping into each other, tripping down stairs and falling over the ottoman trying to get into the car. It wasn't like that at all. It was more like the heady excitement of not wanting to miss the plane that would be taking you on an exotic vacation. The best part was coming soon. All we had to do was to get to the hospital. There, everything would be taken care of for us.

At seven thirty we left for the hospital. We let the dog and cat out; the laundry was clean and folded; the beds were made; the trash was taken out; and the nursery was ready. The last thing we did before we left was take pictures. Claire was patient while I fumbled with the camera and agonized over the best angles and backgrounds, but clearly she was eager to leave. Carrying around thirty pounds of baby, placenta, and amniotic fluid was exhausting. Characteristically, her hands were clasped under her mighty belly, as if the baby would fall out if she let go.

We drove to the hospital together in my car. We were quiet, each of us alone with our private thoughts. There was little traffic in our direction, despite the hour, and at eight a.m. we arrived at the hospital's obstetrics wing, cutely named, "O.B./T.L.C." I wondered how "cute" they'd find our little trio. We were all frightened. Check-in took no time at all; it helped to have pre-registered. We were ushered back to a semi-private examining room where Claire was shown to her bed. Chairs were provided for us. The nurses were surprisingly friendly and accommodating. Had they been alerted to expect our unusual threesome? Did they know Dr. Westrick?

It was then that a feeling of unreality began to flow over me, as if this day, which we had been looking forward to with such intense desire for so long, wasn't really happening. The nurse hooked up the fetal and uterine contraction monitors to Claire. They wanted to make sure that the baby was waking up more and more with each contraction. As soon as we got settled, in strode a smiling Dr. Shelly in full scrubs.

It was comforting to have him in charge. What a relief it was to see his familiar, friendly face. Shelly's first job was to examine Claire to make sure that the baby was still in the vertex position. If he was not, Shelly could not induce labor because he would not be able to deliver Simon vaginally in the breech position. Fortunately, the baby had not changed position since Monday and he was ready to be delivered. Now that the fear of a C-section was behind us, we were ready to proceed.

Shelly held the frozen syringe in his huge fist to thaw it out. It looked like a blue popsicle. He joked about the way he could tell the sex of the baby when he induced labor: he closed his eyes when sticking his hand in the freezer to get out the induction gel. If he pulled out a blue one, it was going to be a boy; a pink one meant it would be a girl. Shelly didn't remember that Claire and I knew the sex of the baby from the sonogram, but Sam didn't.

The popsicle was a frozen dose of the hormone, prostaglandin. Thawed, the gel would stimulate Claire's uterus to begin contracting. The gel was going to soften her cervix and help her to dilate. At precisely eight thirty a.m. Shelly inserted the gel, explaining again that Claire might require another dose to go into full labor. Fumbling with my camcorder and trying to get a good shot while not intruding, I recorded every grimace.

Afterwards, we had nothing to do but wait. We chatted, joked, and read. Claire and I played gin rummy. We laughed when she accused me of cheating. Shelly poked his head in hourly to check on Claire's progress; her nurse was in every ten minutes. I remember thinking, of the thousands of expectant families who went before us, we were probably the only male couple to adopt a baby in this hospital.

By twelve thirty p.m., the monitor revealed that the medicine was working. Claire was starting to go into labor. The contractions were coming regularly, every seven or eight minutes. We could tell by her groans that the contractions were becoming more painful. However, Shelly found Claire was still dilated only one and a half centimeters and not quite in active labor. He gave her another dose to move things along, predicting that she would go into labor soon.

Claire was a trooper, and tolerated the cold gel well. After about an hour, active labor finally began. Each contraction was reflected in a pained expression on Claire's face. The fetal heartbeat and uterine contraction monitors trailed out graph paper like a ticker tape in slow motion. The profile of her contractions on the tape was beginning to look more like regular waves than the intermittent seismic eruptions they had been in the morning. By two p.m. it was time to go to the birthing suite. We were going to deliver a baby, Shelly, Claire, Dad and Daddy!

Claire was asked to walk herself down the hall. I offered my arm and she held on tightly. After we were ensconced in the suite, Shelly came back at two thirty p.m. An I.V. was started and pitocin was dripped into her vein. Pitocin was the drug that would send her over the edge by potentiating the labor contractions that would deliver Simon. By three o'clock Claire had tolerated all the pain she felt she could take and began asking for the anesthetic. "I'm ready for my drugs now," she stated politely. The anesthesiologist was in the next suite attending to another patient and Claire had to wait her turn. After fifteen minutes, however, her request became a command: "I don't care if he is with someone else. Shelly said he wouldn't let me have pain and this HURTS. I WANT MY DRUGS!"

After too long a wait, a smiling, young anesthesiologist loped in and helped us assist Claire into the sitting position so he could administer the epidural. It was morbidly fascinating to watch him work. With both of their permissions, I videotaped the entire procedure. After twenty minutes, his work was done and the anesthetic was starting to work. As we looked at the monitor, we could see the frequency and severity of the contractions, but by three fifteen Claire was feeling no pain. By three thirty she was fully dilated. Incredibly, Claire had gone from one and a half centimeters to ten centimeters in just three hours. That's our birthmother!

Now, Claire was ready to give birth. I positioned myself at the foot of her bed with her left leg braced on my left shoulder. Her legs were dead weight because of the epidural. I supported her left thigh with my left hand and held my camera in my right. I was too caught up in the moment to care about how ridiculous I must have looked. Shelly was seated on a rolling stool in front of her spread-eagled legs and Sam was behind Shelly holding the camcorder. The nurse supported Claire's right thigh and counted out loud, instructing her when to push. Between contractions, Claire asked that a mirror be positioned so that she could see the birth take place. I made sure that the mirror was correctly angled. Again, I found myself fumbling with the damn camera, torn between living the moment as a full participant and recording it as a spectator. I found the middle ground as the few colorful photographs I managed to take later demonstrated.

By four thirty Claire was pushing with every contraction as hard as she could. Finally, we could see the crown of Simon's head. We were all telling her to push when we got our cue from the uterine contraction monitor. I was absolutely swept up in the excitement of the moment. The baby had dark hair. As soon as we could see the top of Simon's head, Shelly attached electrodes so he could monitor his descent down the birth canal and be alert if the baby was in distress. Everything looked good on the monitor. At four thirty-six p.m. Simon's head was fully crowned and it became clear to Shelly that an episiotomy was necessary. The baby was bigger than anyone had expected. After the episiotomy, at four thirty-nine p.m. Simon's entire head was delivered. Shelly immediately suctioned the nose and mouth, even before the neck was out. Then, I saw that the umbilicus was caught around the baby's neck. Shelly told Claire to stop pushing while he unwrapped the cord. That done in an instant, we were home free. One more push and this warm, wet, waxy ball of flesh whooshed out, followed by a flood of liquid. Jumpin' Jehosephat! The floods of Rahjampoor were upon us. For some reason, I thought of Bette Midler and smiled my toothiest, ear-to-ear grin.

The baby was huge, attached to a thick blue cord. It was a boy! A big, beautiful, strapping, healthy boy. Shelly clamped the cord in two places and handed me the scissors. Although our birth plan called for Sam to cut the cord, he was busy videotaping the birth and I was standing right there between Shelly and Claire. I offered the scissors to Sam, but he motioned for me to cut the connection between Simon and his birthmother. I was amazed at how tough the cord was. It required more of a sawing motion with my surgical scissor than an easy snip. Cutting the cord was, for me, the symbolic act of both receiving Simon into our lives and severing his tie to his birthmother.

Once the cut was complete, he was ours, mine and Sam's together. The act was a triumph. I was ecstatic. Claire was exhausted. We were all exhilarated. The nurse, draped in the receiving blanket, swooped in, wrapped the precious bundle up and took him to the warmer (which was not unlike a poultry egg incubator) for his first examination. Simon was pink and healthy and received Apgar scores of eight and nine at one and five minutes. Then, he was taken to the scale, where we saw the pointer go up to ten pounds. A ten pound baby boy! At twenty-one and a half inches he was a giant. We were so happy, so proud of Simon, of Claire, of Shelly, the hospital. This was the happiest moment of my life. I was too exhilarated to appreciate what Claire was probably feeling at that moment.

Claire asked if Simon had all his parts. We assured her that he did and showed her the polaroid pictures we took to prove it. After he was foot-printed, wrist-banded, and had his blood drawn, I was given bottled water to feed him in accordance with our birth plan. But Simon didn't know how to drink. He didn't know how to suck. The nurse said that his sugar was a bit low and that it was important to get him to drink. My first challenge. However long I left the nipple in his mouth, he just wouldn't draw on it. "C'mon, Simon, I intoned, "just a drop for your old Dad. Don't make me look like the total novice that I am!" Finally, he took a few drops. Simon's and Dad's first accomplishment.

After undergoing all the procedures required by hospital routine, Simon was taken to the nursery rather than being placed on his birthmother's belly in accordance with our birth plan. There, I helped to give him his first bath. The nurse showed me how to wash him and shampoo his tiny head. Together, we cleaned off the blood and dried amniotic fluid from his ordeal. He quickly pinked up and looked like the picture of health. Boy, did I feel clumsy handling that little baby. I was lucky to have an experienced nurse show me how.

By this time, it was about six-thirty p.m. Simon was two hours old. I went back to the birthing suite to visit Claire, where I discovered her alert and awake. The only thing that was keeping her from going to her private room was that her right leg was still numb and she couldn't move it. They would release her only after the epidural had worn off. After another hour, she was all right to move, so we gathered up her things and escorted her to her room. We helped her settle in and Sam presented her with a gorgeous bouquet of flowers. We chatted animatedly, reliving the glorious moments surrounding the birth. We congratulated ourselves on a job well done, but no one really wanted the champagne we brought to toast the new arrival. Our triumph was Claire's loss.

Then, Claire asked to see Simon. I froze, hoping she wouldn't detect my fear. I knew we had agreed she could see him any time she wanted, but I didn't want her to bond with him. I imagined this bonding process all the baby books wrote about was similar to the patterning phenomenon in ducklings—they followed the first moving object they saw after hatching, regardless of the species. I was terrified she would change her mind once her eyes locked onto the baby's. There was nothing I could do. He was her baby boy. We were just invited friends.

Simon was wheeled into the room in his trolley bassinet, pink and handsome and robust. I picked him up and gave him, ceremonially, to his birthmother. My heart sank as I momentarily felt like I was losing my new baby. Claire was quite curious, almost clinical in her inspection. She unwrapped his swaddling, looked at his hands and toes and exclaimed that he looked just like her youngest. She held him while we continued to talk. She seemed to enjoy holding him. It grew late and the exhaustion following the events of the day was catching up with us. By eleven p.m., we had to go home. Claire was getting tired, too. She rang for the nurse and said she was ready to have the baby taken back to the nursery. I silently breathed my relief as I saw him wheeled down the hall, back to the safety of the nursery and away from the woman who had just given him life. If Claire was suffering, she did not show it. I was impressed with her stoicism. We left shortly thereafter, hugging and kissing Claire goodnight. I whispered in her ear as I leaned over to kiss her, "Thank you for making my life complete." And that's exactly what this extraordinary woman did for me.

The next morning, Sam and I again awoke at six a.m. so we could be at the hospital by seven-thirty. Claire had said she wanted to leave by eight a.m. so she could be home to her children in time for lunch. Simon was to be examined by the pediatrician at eight and Shelly was going to perform the circumcision after that. We had a busy morning ahead of us.

Instead of going straight to the nursery when we arrived at the hospital, I went to Claire's room. I was concerned about her and didn't want her to think that, now that she had given birth, we no longer cared about her. As I opened the door, I was startled to find Simon in Claire's room. He was in her arms. I could barely hide my fright. I thought she had changed her mind. As if she could read my mind, Claire explained that the nurse had brought Simon in from the nursery at 2:00 a.m. when she said it was feeding time, unsolicited by Claire. She also said that a group of nurses came in during the night oohing and ahhing over the baby saying, "Is this Dr. Westrick's baby?" Claire seemed to feel proud that she was having the baby of a doctor on the staff. She gave no indication that she had changed her mind about the adoption.

The nurse left Simon with Claire all night. I was furious and terrified. I stayed calm, however, and made my best effort not to show how upset I felt. I could not imagine that a nurse would be so insensitive as to leave with a new mother the baby she was planning to give up for adoption. Only later was I to learn that the nurse told

Sam that it was Claire who asked for the baby. The nurse did not bring Simon to Claire on her own. Claire lied to me. Why? Where would this lead?

Sam and I spent the next hour in Claire's room with Simon and Claire until we were told that he was wanted in the nursery for his examination at nursery rounds. We followed the bassinet to the nursery but had to wait outside while rounds were being conducted. It was there that I met our first pediatrician. He pronounced Simon healthy and normal and told us we could take him out of the hospital whenever the legal work was accomplished. Simon was to be discharged less than twenty-four hours after being born. Were we prepared? All of a sudden, I was not so sure.

Immediately after his check-up, Simon was in demand again. This time, from Dr. Shelly, who was ready to perform the circumcision (even though he was against circumcisions). Sam and I had lengthy discussions about whether or not to have this done. We recognized the lack of medical necessity and the fact that the overwhelming majority of males in the world were uncircumcised. However, most Americans were circumcised and we didn't want this child to have any more differences from his peers than already existed. Besides, we wanted him to look like us. Although Jewish, I identified more with the reform branch and did not feel that we had to have this procedure performed ceremonially by a *moyl*. By omitting the *moyl,* I opted out of the conservative Jewish tradition in which I had grown up.

I was ready with the camcorder, but it was a painful procedure to watch. Shelly was careful. He injected an anesthetic before he began. Half-way through, to our surprise, Claire came in to watch as well. She was fully dressed and eager to go home. By now it was clear that Claire had not changed her mind. After the half-hour procedure, the four of us went back to Claire's room where we waited together for Claire, then Simon, to be discharged. All that we needed was a visit from the hospital social worker and signatures on the appropriate forms for the hospital to release Simon to the adoption agency. The attorney was scheduled to come at two p.m. I couldn't believe we were so close to taking our baby home from the hospital.

The social worker finally came just before lunch. She talked with us for a while, had Claire sign the necessary forms, then left. Claire granted our wish to name the baby and just as we intended he was named: Simon Samuel Morgen-Westrick. The social worker was supportive, positive and couldn't have been nicer.

Then, just before lunch, Claire's nurse came in with her discharge instructions. Sam brought her things out to her car, which I had tanked up and driven to the hospital that morning. It was rainy and gray out. Simon was brought back to the nursery. Before he was wheeled out, I asked if Claire wanted to say one last goodbye. She didn't. She had spent her night with him, just she and her baby alone, and said it all in private. She looked away and checked her overnight case as Simon was wheeled from the room. It was a quietly wrenching moment.

We walked Claire out of the hospital and to her car. We hugged and kissed her, urging her to drive safely and to be sure to call us when she got home. By this time it was just drizzling. Tropical storm Danielle had blown itself out off the coast that day. We waved in wonderment as she drove off. A part of me felt like a heel—shouldn't we have arranged for a driver for her? A chauffeur-driven limousine wouldn't have been too good for this angel. But this was the way she wanted it. As Claire pulled away, we waved and she waved back, smiling through her rear-view mirror. She had left behind the greatest gift that any human being can give another.

Could it really be true? Could Simon be ours? His birthmother had gone. We were preparing to bring him home in less than three hours. What joy we felt. But wait, could we really celebrate? Something unexpected could happen. Superstition forbade me to let out the "YAHOO" that was welling up inside me. It felt like all the holidays of my life rolled into one.

We went back to the nursery, where the nurse instructed us on the use of vaseline over the circumcision site and alcohol swabs on the umbilicus. She counseled us that the baby should sleep on his side when we got home, so that he would not choke should he spit up. After he was given his first dose of the Hepatitis B vaccine and his first PKU test he was ready to go. All that was left was for the legal papers to be signed.

The attorney for the adoption agency would be there in an hour. We needed one last item—a car seat. Sam and I made a quick trip to a nearby store and bought one that had a canopy and a detachable base. The number of choices available in the kiddie market was dizzying.

At two p.m., the attorney from the agency strode in and greeted us with a big smile. He said that Simon was an agency record for baby size. He and the hospital social worker exchanged pleasantries and signatures. I introduced him to Simon's other father, Sam, who was also waiting in the nursery. At two-thirty p.m. on Friday, September twenty-fifth, twenty-two hours after his birth, Simon Morgen-Westrick was ours. I could not believe that the years of waiting and wishing, dreaming and hoping were over. We were free to take him home. I could barely comprehend the enormity of the moment. Sam and I looked at each other conspiratorially. Later, in the car, we admitted that we couldn't believe they were letting us take this baby out of the hospital. What did we know about taking care of babies? I thought of Prissy's famous exclamation to Miss Scarlett in that scene from *Gone With the Wind*, "I don't know nothin' 'bout birthin' babies."

The attendant, a middle-aged hospital volunteer, loaded us down with free samples: nipples, formula, pacifiers, and other necessities. She seemed delighted to be helping two men bundle this baby into the car. Sam videotaped us leaving the hospital. Simon was a little bundle of swaddling in my arms. The attendant made sure that he was snug in his new car seat before she hugged us, wished us good luck, and waved goodbye.

By three p.m. we were pulling away from the hospital parking lot. We were taking Simon home at last. My family, our family, together at last. Words fail in describing the relief, the joy, the exhilaration, the terror of that moment. I knew that our lives were irrevocably changed.

My Dear Darling Son,

It's eight-thirty Sunday morning and you are not even three days old. You are nestled asleep in my lap as I write this. Only now is the reality of your presence beginning to sink in. My heart is overflowing with love for you and gratitude to your birthmother for bestowing her trust and confidence on us. I spoke with her yesterday to make sure she was all right and she told me to tell you she loves you.

Looking into your beautiful face, I see the tiny person you are, full of potential, full of life, part of us now until we die. We will discover over the coming years that we are a family—with all the love and commitment and bonding that implies. Our value is in our love for each other.

My promise to you, on this third day of your life, is that I will love you, cherish you and be here for you forever. I am your father, just as Daddy Sam is your other father. I will feed you and shelter you and care for you in sickness and health; I will educate you and enrich your life with all that I have to give; I will work to make you feel secure and competent; I will empower you and try to create an environment for you which will help you to love yourself and be considerate of others; I will respect your feelings and your differences from me, yet I will instill values in your life so that you will be held in esteem by others. All that I have will some day be yours. My family is now your family. Daddy Sam's family is now your family.

You are not an orphan, nor have you ever been. From the moment we knew of your existence—even before your birthmother knew you were inside her, we have been here waiting for you, wanting you, praying you would come to us as you have finally done. Welcome home, darling little son, welcome home.

Dad

Chapter Twenty-Seven

When Simon was four days old, Claire called. She sounded upbeat. She said the adoption agency representative was going to be there in fifteen minutes. Claire had arranged to have the birthfather there as well. She said he was annoyed at having to come at all and might be reluctant to give any more information about himself than his signature on the legal documents. However, it was a wonderful relief that she called; she could still have changed her mind. Claire said she was going in to her office and that she was ready now to go back to work. She denied any further bleeding or abdominal pain, although she indicated that her breasts were now starting to produce milk. If she didn't realize how big a baby Simon was from holding him in the hospital, she knew it now because of the vast quantity of milk she was producing.

Ten days later, the rescission period during which Simon's birthparents could reclaim their parental rights and responsibilities passed uneventfully. Those rights were now relinquished irrevocably and forever. Our petition to adopt was filed on the eleventh day and the next step toward Simon's permanent adoption was completed. All we had to wait for now were three post-placement home visits from the agency and the final decree of adoption six months from the date Simon started living with us.

What an incredible woman Claire was. I regretted not trusting her sooner. When she last called, I did not hear pain or tears in her voice, simply relief that the pregnancy was over and that she had her life and her family back. We talked a bit of business regarding hospital bills, then said goodbye. We would be seeing each other for the last time in six weeks, at her final post-partum check-up and release from her obstetrician's care.

Simon was six weeks old the day I turned forty-two. That was when we had our last meeting with Claire at the doctor's office for her follow-up appointment. I experienced a moment of terror when I fantasized that she would be waiting there with a baby carriage to take Simon back, but it was only a bit of "terriblizing" again.

I arrived at the doctor's office promptly at four p.m. Sam had not yet arrived. I dressed Simon in his best outfit, a blue-striped and polka-dotted affair, that made him look more like a doll than a kid. I thought it would be appealing to Claire and further demonstrate that we were taking good care of him. I still felt the need to prove myself to her. On the way out the door that afternoon, I also took the four-inch stack of greeting cards that we had received in the weeks after Simon's arrival. Still insecure, even after I had Claire's signed relinquishment, I wanted to prove that Simon was welcomed not only into our family, but into our extended family of friends and relatives as well. It would take several months for me to overcome the fear that somehow, someone could come and take Simon away.

I wrapped him in his soft, baby blue blanket—the one with his name embroidered on it—and strode into the waiting room. I immediately saw Claire behind the glass partition with the doctor. All three nurses were also present and, simultaneously, they all broke out into smiles. They had been there throughout the pregnancy and were happy for us. "He's so BIG! How beautiful he is. He's only SIX weeks old?" they exclaimed in disbelief. Claire was smiling, too, and she and Shelly came out to greet us.

Simon was sleeping peacefully in my arms. After showing him off I sat on a sofa in the waiting room. Claire joined me and we began to catch up. Claire looked great. It was the first time I had seen her in eye makeup. She had lost thirty pounds since the beginning of her pregnancy and she was dressed attractively. She seemed happy. I was not at all threatened by her smiles at Simon. The ten day recision period had passed.

I offered him to her. As in the hospital, when I gave him to her after the birth, there was something ritualistic in that act, almost as if I was making a symbolic offering of trust. Simon's birthmother took him in her arms and looked down at him benevolently. Just as she said in the hospital, she said again how much he looked like her youngest child. She appeared content holding him. The holding did not seem to trigger any pain for Claire. And when she had enough, she gave him back with the same mysterious smile.

Sam came into the waiting room shortly thereafter and we traded stories of recent events. Claire looked over our cards with smiles. Then, she gave us pictures and notes for Simon from her other children. I planned to put them carefully away until that day when we discuss the circumstances of his adoption.

From the waiting room, we decided to go to dinner at the same restaurant at which we had eaten after our last obstetrical appointment before the birth. A light rain had just started to fall. Sam and Claire were seated quickly. We were just in time to avoid the early dinner crowd. Simon had awakened and was crying so lustily that I had to feed and comfort him in the car before going in with him to the restaurant to join Sam and Claire.

We sat at a booth and learned that Claire was fine. She was back at her old job and her children were happy to have her home again. She had gone out on a couple of dates and seemed to be renewing her interest in men. I remembered how Claire had said that her therapist had made her see a psychiatrist when she came in for her first appointment after the birth because she had been crying non-stop for days. Claire explained her it as a result of her hormones raging, her uterus contracting and still bleeding heavily and her engorged breasts leaking milk. She felt her whole body was out of control. She said her therapist and the psychiatrist wanted to read too much into her crying. They interpreted her tears as mourning for a lost baby. Today, she denied she was in mourning. And I could see no evidence of grief. Whatever post-partum depression she might have experienced had resolved.

Claire reiterated that she was very happy for Simon and felt he was as lucky to have us as we were to have him. She said that the whole experience was gratifying for her and that, as a mechanism of self-protection, she forgot the painful parts of the pregnancy and delivery. She insisted that she was going to do it again in a year so she could give birth in the summer after next. If we wanted to have another baby then, she would give us "first dibs." Amazed, pleased, but speechless, I mumbled my appreciation. The only stipulation was made plaintively: "Please don't put me through those stupid psychological tests again."

Our goodbyes were said in the parking lot of the Denny's restaurant on Belair Road. We hugged and kissed and there were no tears. We thanked Claire again for giving us Simon and for being our friend. We recognized that we might never see each other again. As was our custom, we drove back to the Baltimore beltway together. I waved one last time to our dear birthmother as she continued north for the long trip home to Pennsylvania. For Simon, Sam, and me, one journey had ended and another had begun. We were a family at last.

We did not plant you. True. But when the season is done—when the alternate prayers for sun and for rain are counted—when the pain of weeding and the pride of watching are through, then we will hold you high, a shining sheaf above the thousand seed grown wild. Not our planting but by heaven, our harvest, our Simon, our own darling child.[1]

---

[1]By permission, adopted from "To An Adopted" from *Beginnings* by Carol Lynn Pearson, Bookcraft, 1967.

Chapter
Twenty-Eight

M any gay and lesbian people whose paths we crossed on our journey to parenthood expressed an interest in doing the same thing. Although the lesbian "baby boom" has been in progress for some time, comparatively few gay male couples have succeeded in creating families for themselves. With the gay rights movement stronger than ever and society becoming more enlightened and tolerant of individual differences, the time has never been more advantageous for male couples to build families. In spite of the AIDS epidemic, gay individuals around the country have been discovering that they have more choices in expressing their lifestyles than ever before. And though it certainly takes money to have and raise children, there are public agencies which require little if any financial investment to pair waiting children with prospective adoptive parents. This chapter is devoted to exploring some ways in which gays or lesbians who want to be parents can create their own families.

In my opinion, most important is the presence of a secure, loving, committed relationship. Opening up a dyad to an infant requires a sense of permanence that can only belong to a relationship over time. I would suggest that couples considering adoption have an established track record as a couple before embarking on this journey. It is also important to have the support of your families and friends as well as qualified professionals in law, medicine and psychology. Before embarking on an alternative journey to parenthood, it is imperative that you educate yourself about the intricacies of adoption procedures in your state. This requires homework—reading, attending classes or workshops and talking with professionals. Appendix IV contains a reading list containing titles which gay men and lesbians who are considering parenthood might find helpful.

Obviously, potential fathers must find a child. For lesbian couples, this usually becomes a matter of deciding which partner will become pregnant (if infertility is not a problem) and where they will find a sperm donor (e.g. friend, sibling, doctor, sperm bank, etc.). For male couples, it usually happens by adoption (foreign or domestic, through an agency—public or private—by independent means or the adoption of a foster child) or by finding a birthmother willing to have your child for you, in a variation of surrogate motherhood.

During the search period, if you choose the independent route, as we did, it is important to throw your net out as far as possible. This is not a time to be shy nor is it for the thin-skinned. Tell as many people as you possibly can that you're looking for a child. Ask friends and family to put the word out. Of all the people you tell, perhaps someone will know someone who's pregnant and looking to give the baby up for adoption. The lucky couple who gets that child might be you. In our search, I wrote flyers and sent them every place I could that had a bulletin board. Advertising definitely helps.

Taking the adoption route requires learning the laws of your state to determine how to comply with the legal requirements. We are lucky in Maryland to have an organization called "Families Adopting Children Everywhere," or FACE. This organization for adoptive families offers courses and workshops on the many aspects of adoption. Another way of learning about how to acquire a child is looking to your local gay and lesbian community center. Many courses with catchy titles such as "Maybe Baby" are springing up at such centers around the country. Retaining a reputable family lawyer who has adoption experience and who is comfortable with gay people is always advisable.

In most states, unrelated couples may not adopt a child together. The adoption must be accomplished by one partner or the other in what is referred to as a single parent adoption. That, however, has started to change and numerous jurisdictions have already successfully accomplished second-parent and co-parent adoptions by unmarried individuals. One must remember that the courts always consider the best interests of the child in rendering their decisions. Some jurisdictions are morbidly homophobic and couples considering adoption would be well-advised to avoid disclosing their orientations. The mere mention of homosexuality in those jurisdictions would be the death knell for an otherwise potentially successful adoption. Remember, once the adoption is finalized by a single parent, you can always go back to court with a petition to accomplish a second-parent adoption by your (and the child's) significant other. Organizations such as the National Lesbian Rights Project and the Lambda Legal Defense and Education Fund have family projects which provide legal assistance to gay and lesbian couples all over the country. These groups have their fingers on the pulse of the latest decisions breaking around the country.

Many states have laws regulating independent or private adoptions. These are adoptions in which the birth-parents and adoptive parents meet each other without the assistance of an agent: by word of mouth, advertising, etc. These states allow such adoptions to take place as long as all parties are represented by legal counsel. In Maryland, as in most states, the only expenses adoptive parents may pay for the birthmother are legal and medical expenses.

Other adoptions occur with the assistance of a licensed private adoption agency. Such an agency may locate a child and process all the paperwork or it may fulfill a smaller role, e.g., taking care of the paperwork for parties who locate a child themselves, known as an agency-assisted adoption. International adoption is another option. Support and education organizations such as the Latin American Parents Association have sprung up to assist prospective adoptive parents in locating an international child. In our case, talking with other members of the Association for Single Adoptive Parents was particularly helpful at the beginning of our journey.

Generally, the fees involved in using a licensed private adoption agency become higher as the level of service increases. At the time of this writing, a home study (which is a prerequisite for any adoption) from such an agency costs approximately one thousand dollars. Handling the paperwork, if you locate the baby yourself, adds thirty-five hundred dollars to the bill. Post-placement home visits add yet another nine hundred dollars plus expenses. If the agency locates the child for you, the costs could quadruple.

For those considering surrogacy, the waters in this territory are barely charted. Few states regulate such contracts, making written agreements unenforceable in court and thus, they are more like written gentleman's agreements. In many states, surrogate mother contracts are against public policy. In some, they are against the law. Even if unenforceable, the surrogate mother contract is a good idea if you plan to go that route so that each party involved can fully understand the scope of his/her commitment. Appendix III contains suggestions as to what should be included in a surrogate mother contract for gay couples. This information was amalgamated from a variety of published and unpublished sources. The list is not comprehensive and serves only as an example of the issues needing to be addressed in such an agreement. Competent legal counsel is a must for all parties involved in a surrogate motherhood agreement.

In my research into this field, I discovered that surrogate mother clinics in New York and California accept only applicants who have already given birth. These women know what it's like to be pregnant, know how their hormones and bodies change, and know what to anticipate as the pregnancy progresses and the birth comes. Only women who have already given birth to children can truly give informed consent. This is certainly something to keep in mind when considering the adventurous route of going with a surrogate mother.

Of the agencies whose representatives I have interviewed, most say that surrogate mothers select themselves. As a psychologist, I was fortunate in having the professional ability to screen applicants. I would likewise recommend that serious applicants be screened psychologically to rule out the presence of psychopathy or sociopathy. Applicants also need to be represented by their own counsel and screened obstetrically.

The fees for a surrogate mother, on top of legal and medical expenses, generally start at ten thousand dollars and may run much higher. Fees may also include additional payment for replacement of lost wages from work if the birthmother is disabled or put on bed-rest. Travel, maternity clothes, and other incidental expenses of a pregnancy and delivery can add yet more cost. Some contracts also require inclusion of life insurance for the birthmother, with either her children or family named as beneficiaries. Not to be confused with baby-buying, surrogacy requires payment for services ren-dered: undergoing screening, artificial insemination, the preg-nancy, exams, tests and treatments during the pregnancy and the labor and delivery of the child.

Gay male couples must also decide whose sperm will be used. One should not overlook the possibility of using a mixture of the couple's semen. Although only one father's sperm can fertilize an egg, some gay male couples might view such a milk shake as the nearest thing to producing their own child.

Perhaps the single most important thing to remember is that if you want a child badly enough and devote as much of your creativity and energy to the task as possible, you will succeed. Even though there will likely be numerous obstacles and disappointments, these typify the experiences of prospective adoptive parents of either gender or sexual orientation—dues to be paid to accomplish one of the greatest joys in life: raising a child. Good luck!

Epilogue

A robust, easy baby, Simon outgrew his clothing about as fast as it could be replaced. By the end of his first year, he was the size of an average three year old. At two, he wore four year olds' clothing. His health has been excellent. Sam's and my plan to parent him without assistance has worked out exceedingly well so far. When Simon was three months old, we joined a lesbian and gay parents and kids' play group.

Before Simon was eight months old, he had become a seasoned traveller. We flew frequently, showing him off at every opportunity at such faraway places as San Francisco, Key West, Palm Springs, Laguna Beach and San Diego. Perhaps one of the most exciting and momentous events in our short family history, however, was the April '93 March on Washington for Lesbian, Gay and Bi Rights. Simon became a part of history that day as the three of us marched in the stroller brigade with hundreds of other gay and lesbian parents with their children. "Two-Four-Six-Eight Not All Moms and Dads Are Straight" was the chant that day.

Our only unfortunate experience came unexpectedly from one of Sam's closest relations—a couple who were fundamentalist Christians. Their absence at a family holiday dinner in protest of our presence and their alleged verbal denigration of our family serve as an ugly reminder of the hypocrisy of the religious right and religious extremists' ability to contradict and undermine the very family values they espouse.

The final decree of adoption was issued when Simon was seven months old. What a relief it was to receive that piece of paper. When he was home free, we turned our attention to other important matters, like our plan to adopt a little brother for Simon. That plan became a reality twenty-three months after Simon's miraculous birth. Now, we are a family of four.

Appendix I

APPLICATION TO BECOME
A SURROGATE MOTHER

Date: _____

INSTRUCTIONS:

Please attach recent photograph to this application. If married, include a photograph of your husband and children. Answer all questions in your own handwriting. All information will be verified and kept confidential. Answer all questions. If the question is not applicable, write "N/A." By signing below, you hereby give permission to obtain a credit report of your financial history.

Name: _____

Address: _____

DOB/Age: (yours) _____ (spouse's) _____

Telephone number: (home) _____ (work) _____

Social Security number: (yours) _____

(spouse's) _____

Employer: _____

Work address/telephone: _____

Health Insurance (name and address of carrier):

_____

_____

_____

    policy no.: _____

    ID: _____

    Group name/no.: _____

    effective date: _____

    name of subscriber: _____

    relationship to subscriber: _____

    employer of subscriber: _____

Marital status: _____

Spouse's name: _____

Spouse's address (if different): _____

_____

Spouse's Employer: _____

Work address: _____

_____

Your monthly income & source: _____

Spouse's monthly income & source: _____

Types, amounts of public assistance, if applicable:

_____

_____

_____

List in chronological order the dates and reasons you have consulted an attorney and/or appeared in court, if applicable (please remember a background check will be performed). Is there anything in your legal background which will show up that you would like to explain here?

_____

_____

_____

_____

_____

List the dates and reasons you have been arrested and/or incarcerated, if applicable.

_____

_____

_____

List the names and dates, in chronological order, of mental health professionals (social workers, mental health counselors, psychologists and/or psychiatrists, etc.) and inpatient or outpatient treatment programs, clinics, hospitals or mental health practices where you have had evaluation and/or treatment:

_____

_____

_____

_____

_____

Religion: _____ Practicing? _____

Parents' names: _____

Mother's address: _____

Father's address: _____

Telephone numbers: (mother): _____ (father): _____

Siblings' names, addresses, telephone numbers:

_____

_____

_____

_____

Children's names and dates of birth:

_____

_____

_____

_____

Three references (please include one professional):

Name   Address   Tel. #   Relationship

1. _____
2. _____
3. _____

On a separate sheet, please answer each of the following questions in as much detail as possible:

1. Why do you want to become a surrogate mother?

2. How does being pregnant affect you? Discuss the pleasant and unpleasant aspects of pregnancy in detail.

3. Discuss the gay men or lesbians you know and your feelings about them.

4. How do you imagine it will be different for a child to grow up in a gay male household as opposed to a traditional one?

5. How do you anticipate your pregnancy will impact on your husband, child(ren), friends, extended family and co-workers?

6. How and when do you intend to tell your family and friends that you are planning on giving the baby up for adoption?

7. Describe the role babies play in your life.

8. Do you anticipate bonding with the baby before it's born? After? Describe the relationship you anticipate with such a baby during the pregnancy.

9. Would you be willing to write a letter to the baby before it is born to be given to him or her at a certain age? What would you want to say in such a letter?

10. What do you believe your religion teaches about surrogacy?

11. What gives you confidence that you will be able to relinquish the baby after it's born? How do you anticipate you will feel?

12. a) Describe how have you felt about each abortion and/or miscarriage you might have had in the past. b) How would you feel about having an abortion if the fetus was seriously abnormal enough to medically warrant it?

13. What will you do with the money you make from being a surrogate mother?

14. Discuss in detail your feelings about the Baby M case (the surrogate mother who changed her mind and fought a legal battle).

15. How do you think you'll be different from Marybeth Whitehead?

16. Have you previously been a surrogate mother or given any children up for adoption? If so, describe in detail.

17. What would be the best type and frequency of prenatal contact with the biological father and his partner during the pregnancy (e.g. weekly, monthly, with each doctor's appointment, etc.)?

18. Whom would you like to have in the delivery room with you?

19. Who is your obstetrician/gynecologist (name, address, phone)?

20. Would you like to have your obstetrician/gynecologist attend you or would you consent to a doctor chosen by the biological/ adoptive fathers?

21. Describe in detail what contact, if any, you would like with the child/ren after birth. With the adoptive parent.

22. Would you undergo an amniocentesis?

23. Discuss any other concerns or questions you have about being a surrogate mother.

Signature _____

Date _____

Return completed questionnaire to:

(Your name and address)

Appendix II

SAMPLE BIRTH PLAN

BIRTH PLAN OF (Names of birthmother and adoptive parent/s)

_____

Date _____

Birth plans should contain statements of the adoptive and birth-parents' wishes about the following concerns of childbirth; should be addressed to both the obstetrician and the hospital; and should be included in the birthmother's chart:

1) Pain Medication

2) Episiotomy

3) Room Request. [Always request a private room for a birthmother who intends to relinquish her parental rights]

4) Caesarian section [Especially note who should be present, if this becomes necessary]

5) Photography/videography

6) Others in the birthing room

7) Immediately after birth [Who will cut the cord? To whom will the baby be given? Who will bathe and feed the child as normal routine permits? Will the baby room in with its birthmother or stay in the hospital nursery?]

8) Who will be present for the weighing of the baby, the administration of eye drops, the pediatric exam, and the baby's first bath?

9) What should **not** happen, e.g. the baby should generally **not** be placed on the birthmother's stomach after birth if she is going to give it up for adoption. Such a birthmother should generally **not** room-in with another woman who has just given birth but will be keeping her baby.

10) Visitors

12) Medical decisions

13) Medical releases signed by birthmother to adoptive parents

14) Birthmother's consent to nursery information and admission to the adoptive parent/s

15) Circumcision

Appendix III

**SUGGESTED ITEMS FOR INCLUSION
IN A CONTRACT TO HAVE A BABY
BY A SURROGATE MOTHER**

Date
Definitions
Descriptions of the parties
Understanding of the medical/legal/psychological risks involved
Diseases associated with pregnancy
Physical and mental evaluations of the parties, including HIV, VD,
    and obstetrical
Life insurance for the parties
Prenatal care
Surrogate mother's not smoking, drinking or taking non-prescrip-
    tion drugs
Release of all pertinent information to the biological father
Conditions under which the pregnancy may be terminated
Amniocentesis and other prenatal testing
Abortion
If the biological father dies before the child is born
Labor and delivery plans, e.g. birth plan
Timing and manner of executing legal documents after the birth
Paternity testing
Counseling before and/or after the birth

If the child is not born healthy
Financial considerations
Contingency for unsuccessful completion of the pregnancy. e.g., miscarriage, stillbirth, or therapeutic abortion
Confidentiality
Cancelling the contract
Breach of contract
Understanding that there are no guarantees
Recognition of existing pertinent laws
Enforceability of contract
Severability clause
Signatures of all parties concerned

Appendix IV

RECOMMENDED READINGS PERTAINING TO GAY/LESBIAN ADOPTION AND SURROGACY

Andrews, Lori B. *Between Strangers: Surrogate Mothers, Expectant Fathers, and Brave New Babies*. Harper and Row, New York, 1989.

_____. *New Conceptions: A Consumer's Guide to the Newest Infertility Treatments, including* in Vitro *Fertilization, Artificial Insemination, and Surrogate Motherhood*. Ballantine Books, New York, 1985.

Back, Gloria E. *Are You Still My Mother? Are You Still MY Family?* Warner Books, New York, 1985.

Barret, Robert L., and Robinson, Bryan E. *Gay Fathers*. Lexington Books, Lexington, 1990.

Benkov, Laura. *Reinventing the Family: The Emerging Story of Lesbian and Gay Parents*. Crown, New York, 1994.

Bosche, Susanne. *Jenny Lives with Eric and Martin*. Gay Men's Press, London, 1981.

Bozett, Frederick W., ed. *Gay and Lesbian Parents*. Praeger, New York, 1987.

_____, ed. *Homosexuality and the Family*. Harrington Park Press, Binghamton, 1990.

Brodzinsky, David, and Schechter, Marshall D., eds. *The Psychology of Adoption.* Oxford University Press, New York, 1990.

Center Kids. *The Lesbian and Gay Adoption Resource List.* Lesbian and Gay Community Services Center, 208 West 13th St., New York, NY 10011 ($12.00).

D'Augelli, Anthony R., and Patterson, Charlotte J., eds. *Lesbian, Gay, and Bisexual Identities Over the Lifespan.* Oxford University Press, New York, 1995.

Eisenberg, Arlene, et al. *What to Expect When You're Expecting.* Workman Publishing, New York, 1991.

Elwin, Rosamund, and Paulse, Michele. *Asha's Mums.* Women's Press, Toronto, 1990.

Galloway, Priscilla. *Jennifer Has Two Daddies.*

Gantz, Joe. *Whose Child Cries. Children of Gay Parents Talk About Their Lives.* Jalmar Press, Rolling Hills Estates, 1983.

Gil de Lamadrid, Maria, ed. *Lesbians Choosing Motherhood: Legal Implications of Donor Insemination and Co-Parenting.* National Center for Lesbian Rights, San Francisco, 1991.

Gilman, Lois. *The Adoption Resource Book.* Third ed., HarperPerennial, New York, 1992.

Green, Beverly, and Herek, Gregory, eds. *Contemporary Perspectives on Gay and Lesbian Psychology.* Sage Publications, Newbury Park, CA, 1994.

Green, W. Dorsey, and Clunis, Merliee. *Lesbian Parenting.* The Seal Press, Seattle, Washington, 1995.

Hanscombe, Gillian E., and Forster, Jackie. *Rocking the Cradle.* Alyson Publications, Boston, 1987.

Hayden, Curry, and Clifford, Denis. *A Legal Guide for Lesbian and Gay Couples.* Nolo Press, Berkeley, 1991.

Heron, Ann, and Maran, Meredith. *How Would You Feel If Your Dad Was Gay?* Alyson Publications, Boston, 1991.

Krementz, Jill. *How It Feels to be Adopted.* Alfred A. Knopf, New York, 1982.

Lindsay, Jeanne Warren. *Open Adoption: A Caring Option.* Morning Glory Press, Buena Park, CA, 1987.

Marindin, Hope, ed. *The Handbook for Single Adoptive Parents.* Committee for Single Adoptive Parents, P.O. Box 15084, Chevy Chase, MD 20815.

Martin, April. *The Lesbian and Gay Parenting Handbook: Creating and Raising Our Families.* HarperCollins, New York, 1993.

Melina, Lois Ruskai. *Raising Adopted Children: A Manual for Adoptive Parents.* HarperPerennial, New York, 1979.

_____. *Making Sense of Adoption: A Parent's Guide.* HarperPerennial, New York, 1989.

Michelman, Stanley B., and Schneider, Meg, with Antonia van der Meer. *The Private Adoption Handbook: A Step-by-Step Guide to the Legal, Emotional, and Practical Demands of Adopting a Baby.* Villard Books, New York, 1988.

Newman, Leslea. *Belinda's Bouquet.* Alyson Publications, Boston, 1991.

_____. *Gloria Goes to Gay Pride.* Alyson Publications, Boston, 1991.

_____. *Heather Has Two Mommies.* Alyson Publications, Boston, 1989.

Noble, Elizabeth. *Having Your Baby by Donor Insemination.* Houghton Mifflin, Boston, 1987.

Overvold, Amy. *Surrogate Parenting.* Pharos Books, New York, 1988.

Patterson, Charlotte J. Children of the Lesbian Baby Boom Behavioral Adjustment, Self-concepts and Sex Role Identity. In B. Greene and G. Herek (Eds.), *Lesbian and Gay Psychology* (pp. 156-175). Sage Publications, Thousand Oaks, California, 1994.

_____. Children of Lesbian and Gay Parents. *Child Development, 63,* 1025-1042.

Pies, Cheri. *Considering Parenthood: A Workbook for Lesbians.* Spinsters/Aunt Lute, San Francisco, 1988.

Plumez, Jacquieline Horner. *Successful Adoption.* Harmony Books, New York, 1987.

Pollack, Sandra, and Vaughn, Jean, eds. *Politics of the Heart: A Lesbian Parenting Anthology.* Firebrand Books, Ithaca, 1987.

Rafkin, Louise, ed. *Different Mothers.* Cleis Press, Pittsburgh, 1990.

Rappaport, Bruce. *The Open Adoption Book: A Guide to Adoption Without Tears.* Macmillan, New York, 1992.

Rosenberg, Elinor B. *The Adoption Life Cycle: The Children and Their Families Through the Years.* The Free Press, New York, 1992.

Schulenberg, Joy. *Gay Parenting: A Complete Guide for Gay Men and Lesbians with Children.* Doubleday, New York, 1985.

Shettles, Landrum B., and Rorvik, David. *How to Choose the Sex of Your Baby: A Complete Update on the Method Best Supported by the Scientific Evidence.* Doubleday, New York, 1989.

Silber, Kathleen, and Speedlin, Phylis. *Dear Birthmother.* Corona, San Antonio, 1983.

Sullivan, Michael R. *Adopt the Baby You Want.* Simon and Schuster, New York, 1990.

Valentine, Johnny. *Daddy Machine.* Alyson Publications, Boston, 1992.

____. *Duke Who Outlawed Jelly Beans.* Alyson Publications, Boston, 1991.

Weston, Kath. *Families We Choose.* Columbia University Press, New York, 1991.

Willhoite, Michael. *Daddy's Roomate.* Alyson Publications, Boston, 1990.

____. *Families: A Coloring Book.* Alyson Publications, Boston, 1991.